MONEY PROBLEMS, MARRIAGE SOLUTIONS

MONEY PROBLEMS, MARRIAGE SOLUTIONS

7 KEYS TO ALIGNING YOUR FINANCES AND UNITING YOUR HEARTS

CHUCK BENTLEY

WITH ANN BENTLEY

MOODY PUBLISHERS

CHICAGO

Edited by Elizabeth Cody Newenhuyse
Interior design: Ragont Design
Cover design: Dean Renninger
Cover image of piggy bank copyright © 2017 by maxicam / Shutterstock (125032343). All rights reserved.
Author Photo: Alyssa Scott Photography

Library of Congress Cataloging-in-Publication Data

Names: Bentley, Chuck, author.
Title: Money problems : marriage solutions : seven keys to aligning your finances and uniting your hearts / Chuck Bentley with Ann Bentley.
Description: Chicago : Moody Publishers, [2017] | Includes bibliographical references.
Identifiers: LCCN 2017024074 (print) | LCCN 2017033274 (ebook) | ISBN 9780802495792 | ISBN 9780802415875
Subjects: LCSH: Marriage--Religious aspects--Christianity. | Money--Religious aspects--Christianity. | Wealth--Religious aspects--Christianity.
Classification: LCC BV835 (ebook) | LCC BV835 .B4435 2017 (print) | DDC 248.8/44--dc23
LC record available at https://lccn.loc.gov/2017024074

We hope you enjoy this book from Moody Publishers. Our goal is to provide high-quality, thought-provoking books and products that connect truth to your real needs and challenges. For more information on other books and products written and produced from a biblical perspective, go to www.moodypublishers.com or write to:

Moody Publishers
820 N. La Salle Boulevard
Chicago, IL 60610

3 5 7 9 10 8 6 4 2

Printed in the United States of America

We dedicate this book to our beloved children
and grandchildren:

Charles Henry Bentley III—"Hank"—and Lindsay Bentley
Charles "Henry" Bentley IV
Miles Lewis Bentley
Etta Liora Bentley
Rye Lynford Bentley
Todd Wagner Bentley
John Christian Bentley
Luke David Bentley

May God bless you and your families.
We pray that you will benefit from the lessons we learned
from our mistakes and, more importantly, our victories.

You are our greatest earthly treasure.

CONTENTS

Peace, Then Prosperity

"IT IS IMPOSSIBLE to prosper when there is war. You must seek peace *first*; then you will prosper."

That's what a wise senior business leader counseled me when I asked him for advice to help me solve a problem I faced in our company, a problem that was dragging down the growth of our business. His insight immediately opened my eyes to the solution, and I went and made peace with my adversarial customer. Once that was accomplished, our energies were refocused on growing the company. The advice worked.

But more importantly, I realized that this approach has direct application to our marriages. Oftentimes, we are passively—or aggressively—in conflict with our spouse. We have not sought to make peace and thus are failing to reach the full potential of our marriages because of the lack of unity. This lack of unity directly relates to our financial struggles and impacts our every decision or inability to make a decision together. From this insight, I began to study the powerful benefits of a couple that is at peace with each other, unified and making financial decisions together. Here is the bottom line of what I learned.

9

LOVE, MONEY, AND UNITY

Marriage is not the cause of our financial problems; in fact, it is the very best solution to our financial problems.[1] Surprised? Shocked? You shouldn't be. This truth is supported by study after study.

Research indicate that married people experience less poverty and more prosperity than any other living arrangement, including being single or living together.[2] *New York Times* columnist David Leonhardt cites analysis showing that marriage is part of a "success sequence" that increases one's likelihood of thriving economically, socially, and even physically.[3] The higher the commitment to marriage, and particularly faithfulness in marriage, the more likely a couple is to flourish financially.[4] I have provided extensive support for the many benefits of marriage in the appendix: A Case for Marriage and Families. But there is also a great paradox: money is often cited as the greatest area of frustration, fighting, arguments, stress, and unhappiness, as well as causing the breakup of many marriages. In other words, it is the root source for many mini-wars in our homes.

We have set out to address this tension, which is also an often hidden opportunity. Our desire is to help you flourish financially and, more importantly, to rediscover your love for one another so that you can work together in unity. To do so, we must be frank and transparent about the challenges you will face and the steps needed to overcome the fighting and frustration that rob you of your ability to work together.

Right about now, you're probably expecting me to tell you to cut up the credit cards, get out of debt, and save an unrealistic amount of your income. Not so fast. This is where our approach is unique. We want to help you to join your hearts and minds together—to stop attacking *each other*—to make lasting peace first; then we will help you attack the *financial challenges* as a unified team. This is an approach that will actually work! Many couples I have counseled mistakenly believe that two practical and commonly recommended tools will solve their financial challenges: a financial plan and a budget. These tools are indeed critical to the *mechanics* of managing money. We will talk about them both in depth. But here is the problem—couples can have a great financial plan and a solid budget but still be worlds apart in their heart and mind. If financial plans and budgets alone could transform a man and woman into one, then rich people, financial planners, highly disciplined, or frugal people would likely never divorce or fight about money. But these tools are *external* solutions that do not address the *internal* problems causing the division, strife, dysfunction, and loneliness.

> COUPLES CAN HAVE A GREAT FINANCIAL PLAN AND A SOLID BUDGET BUT STILL BE WORLDS APART IN THEIR HEART AND MIND.

Let me emphasize again that marriage *increases* your likelihood of escaping poverty and experiencing affluence. Your marriage is not the cause of your financial struggles—it is actually the solution! Marriage was designed by God to bring abundant blessing into our lives as we work together in unity as husband and wife, and we believe unity is possible for every couple willing to do the hard work it requires. Yet, millions of couples don't experience these benefits. Is it any mystery why such a barrage of destructive forces is directed at the unity of a marriage, especially in the area of financial decisions? Make no mistake, your financial well-being as a couple is a prime target of Satan. The reality is that we need both love and money, and we need to know how to manage each. The good news is that God gave us everything we need to make both work for a lifetime. There is hope for every marriage, no matter how many winds of conflict and division have attacked or how much damage has been done.

FROM THE ASHES: OUR STORY

Our decision to write this book together was not born from our relational or financial perfection. Make no mistake about it: we are a work in progress. Like most couples, we started off with great optimism, expecting to make the other's life better, not worse; richer, not poorer. But financial mistakes, arguments, fights, stress, misunderstandings, and hurt feelings created division that led to dysfunction and ongoing cycles of emotional, financial, and relational pain. These seemed like no great challenges at first, but they became squalls—ominous, threatening storms. They robbed us of peace in our marriage and progress in our finances. At times, the intensity of the problems threatened to destroy us.

During our thirty-seven years of marriage, Ann and I have experienced significant challenges with each other that on the surface had to do with money. I struggled to even pay our utility bills on time. Ann was once faced with uniformed workers coming to our door to turn off our utilities because of my negligence. But that was just the beginning of more financial pain to come and more serious challenges to contend with. Excessive use of credit cards, risky business loans, job loss, and foolish spending marked my management of our family finances for the next twenty years. On top of the financial insecurity, the situation was extremely challenging for Ann emotionally. She lost a lot of respect for me, questioning my judgment and my failure to properly care for her and our family. But most of the pain and frustration we faced were not caused by financial problems but our lack of alignment and unity in this area—we were stuck!

Peter advises us, "Be alert and of sober mind. Your enemy the devil prowls around like a roaring lion looking for someone to devour" (1 Peter 5:8). We must take this imposter of a roaring lion seriously because these threats are coming from our very real enemy. By God's mercy and grace we began to recognize these attacks and equip ourselves to squelch their power to destroy us. We gradually became united, aligned our finances, and began to make choices according to God's principles, choices that have served to strengthen and bless our family.

And after twenty-one years, peace and unity started to take hold in our marriage. Yes, we endured twenty-one years of division and strife. But as we persevered, wisdom was born out of the pain, beauty rose from the ashes, and the original brightness of our love blossomed. Christ has fulfilled His promise to work all things together for good; Ann and I have forged a united marriage filled with peace, joy, intimacy, and financial health. And our hearts' desire is for you to experience these same benefits in your marriage.

My own failures, weaknesses, and lessons learned have given me a compassionate heart to serve others in this area. God led me to become the CEO of the world's largest Christian financial ministry, Crown Financial Ministries (crown.org). I have personally counseled or taught thousands of couples worldwide who are struggling with the same issues Ann and I have faced in our marriage. Our experiences have given me many opportunities to bring hope to couples who have been under attack relationally, spiritually, and financially. These attacks happen to us all to some degree or another—they are equal-opportunity destroyers. I have seen couples overcome these attacks and successfully get on the same page in every sense. God is truly the God of miracles and redemption. We have lived these words written by Paul: "Praise be to the God and Father of our Lord Jesus Christ, the Father of compassion and the God of all comfort, who comforts us in all our troubles, so that we can comfort those in any trouble with the comfort we ourselves receive from God" (2 Cor. 1:3–4).

THE SEVEN KEYS

As we've mentioned, to align their finances, couples must first be of one heart and mind. Often, we simply are feeling our way through the dark with no clear instruction on how to become united on issues related to money. We simply drag our past training or preferred method into the relationship and move forward. Some think getting debt free will solve all their financial woes. While this may be effective, in some cases I have seen it divide couples and bring more division. Our process consists of seven keys to ensure that couples are united *internally* and the finances are aligned *externally* as a result. The keys can be summarized in seven words, each starting with the letter P: Peacemaker, Prosperity, Purpose, Philosophy, Personality, Plan, and Process.

Each key will address a specific challenge that brings confusion and pain into our marriages and finances. Each of the keys is important and should not be skipped. At the end of the book, I will ask you each to sign Our Money and Marriage Vow to seal your commitment to apply these seven keys. This is a proven process that we have had the privilege of teaching to couples around the world. Begin praying for God to open your own heart to learn and apply these keys, beginning with Peacemaker. Even if your spouse currently has no interest in reading this book or working together on the problem, don't be discouraged. God will use your personal investment in this effort to help you wherever you are.

HOPE FOR ALL

Ann and I truly want you to be free of the fights, arguments, strife, loneliness, rejection, fear, stress, and financial pain that have caused you to pick up this book. Whether you are experiencing these struggles in your own marriage, striving to avoid them, are engaged and not yet married, or are concerned about someone else's marriage, we ask that you allow the Holy Spirit to speak to your heart as you work through each chapter. We want you to be able to identify the real enemy behind these attacks and be equipped with a means to achieve victory over them. Although at times it has been a tough and sometimes painful road for us, we know that anyone can do it! We continue to work on our unity and alignment in our financial decisions together. We hope you will too.

Our prayer is that you will not be another statistic of a failed or frustrated marriage. We believe that by reading this book you will learn to recognize and overcome the obstacles in your way and make financial progress by eliminating the root causes. And if you are a spouse whose marriage has been broken, may God give you insight into what went wrong, mend your broken heart, and reconcile you to your former spouse or restore your own joy and confidence.

Ann has elected to be the silent voice in this book. That is what she preferred. She provided lots of input and ideas in each chapter but specifically added her touch to the practical exercises in chapter 9 and in the appendix that will help you put these lessons into practice.

We think it is time that money no longer be a leading cause for couples to be discouraged, divided, or destroyed. Regardless of where you are now, there is hope ahead. As Desmond Tutu once said, "Hope is being able to see that there is light, despite all of the darkness."

CHUCK AND ANN BENTLEY
Knoxville, Tennessee, USA

CHAPTER ONE

Key #1: Commit to Becoming a Peacemaker

Blessed are the peacemakers,
for they shall be called sons of God.

MATTHEW 5:9 ESV

Make every effort to keep the unity of
the Spirit through the bond of peace.

EPHESIANS 4:3

BY THE TIME we were living in our second home, the one we decided to stretch our budget to buy, Ann and I were experiencing regular conflict over our finances. By any standard, we were "house poor," meaning we were living in a nice home, but it was taking a disproportionate amount of our income to make the payments. There was little to no margin in our finances. Ann wanted to save money, pay down the mortgage, and get prepared to have children. I wanted the same lifestyle our friends seemed to have, even though it was not affordable. They drove new cars, took nice vacations, and were constantly improving their homes. My solution was to borrow more and more money. In my mind, I was being "creative." In Ann's eyes,

I was being "foolish." I thought I was pushing for a better life for our family. In Ann's view, I was simply driven to keep up with our more affluent friends. Of course, these vastly different views created conflict when it came to our budget and spending. Ann was silently suffering fear and insecurity.

What to do?

A woman of our acquaintance points to one solution. "My husband and I used to have these wrenching fights about money that never solved anything," she said. "Very accusing, very doom-and-gloom, very predictable. Our finances at the time were really tight. But in time it dawned on both of us that we had to solve *us* before we could solve our money issues. Our marriage was healthy enough, but the main thing was we needed to approach our finances with love, unity, and mutual respect. When we started doing that, our finances didn't initially change—but *we* did. That's when we started to make real progress."

No couple can escape differences, disagreements, or avoid hurting one another. But what can be avoided is the destruction that often results from unresolved, seemingly never-ending conflict. This cycle of conflict can lurk in a marriage, steal our peace, and wreck our ability to work together on the financial problems.

DIVORCE AND MONEY ARGUMENTS

In a 2012 government-sponsored academic study, researchers examined data related to what couples argue about—including children, money, in-laws, and spending time together—and then looked at which of those couples were divorced four to five years later. According to an article about the study, financial arguments were the leading area of disagreement to predict divorce for both men and women.[1] "In the study, we controlled for income, debt and net worth," lead researcher Sonya Britt said. "Results revealed it didn't matter how much you made or how much you were worth. Arguments about money are the top predictor for divorce because it happens at all levels."[2]

Britt's research provides even more insights about the toll that constant conflict over money takes on our marriages: a) it takes longer to recover from money arguments than any other kind of argument; b) money arguments are more intense; and c) couples often use harsher language with each other, and the argument lasts longer. Britt also noted a very important correlation between relational conflicts and the financial consequences: "By continuing to have financial arguments, couples decrease their relationship satisfaction." The article adds, "Aside from a negative effect on children, increased stress leads to a further decrease in financial planning that could help better the situation."[3]

In August 2013, 191 Certified Divorce Financial Analyst professionals from across North America responded to the following question: "According to what your divorcing clients have told you, what is the main reason that most of them are getting (or have gotten) divorced?" The resulting study identifies the three leading causes of divorce as "basic incompatibility" (43 percent), "infidelity" (28 percent), and "money issues" (22 percent). "Many couples lack the communication skills necessary to navigate financial disagreements in their marriage," noted one respondent. "The emotional connection of money with safety and security in many people makes the financial disagreements more salient than other disagreements." Also, according to this article, "several of the CDFA professionals surveyed noted that the most commonly cited cause of divorce they hear from their clients—'basic incompatibility'—is usually created by deeper issues somewhere in the relationship—usually an emotional, physical, or financial breach of trust."[4]

Additionally, in a recent poll conducted by DivorceMagazine .com, the leading cause of divorce was found to be *financial issues*, followed closely by basic incompatibility. "During the divorce, the two most contentious issues are usually finances and children—in that order," says Dan Couvrette, publisher of *Divorce Magazine*. "If there are no children, then basic incompatibility and communication problems follow on the heels of money problems."[5]

So if money is the root cause of many divorces, a proven plan that goes beyond the typical solutions to help couples safeguard their marriages is long overdue.

WHEN CHOICES LEAD TO CONFLICT

When couples are in a dating relationship, they make any number of small decisions such as where to eat, what movie to see, or what music to listen to together. Most couples enjoy discovering all the things they agree on and often delight in learning about their differences. But marriage requires that couples make decisions together, lots and lots of decisions about a wide range of things such as the brand of toothpaste they buy, the color of their bath towels, where to buy groceries, which Internet provider to use, where to live, which doctors to see, what to have for dinner, how much to spend on entertainment, and which parents to visit for the holidays. When children arrive in the marriage, the weight and complexity of a couple's decisions increases dramatically. The myriad of decisions and choices faced by couples create endless potential for friction. As a couple wrestles with all these choices, they discover their vast differences, and the ensuing disagreements reveal sensitivities previously unknown. Some disagreements are relatively benign . . . has this ever happened to you?

Me: "Where do you want to eat after church?"

Ann: "Oh, I don't care, you pick it."

Me: "Okay, let's get Chinese food."

Ann: "Hmm . . . I don't really want Chinese food today."

Me: "I thought you said I could pick where we eat?"

Ann: "Sure. Go ahead. I just don't want Chinese food. Okay?"

Me: "No problem, let's pick up some burgers . . . "

Ann: "Umm . . ."

Me: "Okay, then you pick!"

Ann: "Let's just fix something at home."

Me: "So, can't we just stick with the original plan?!"

This is a harmless example—but often this lack of unity is exposed through confronting much bigger issues, involving much higher potential costs to the family.

Being able and willing to work through conflict is a vital skill for a successful marriage. This conflict and the resulting pain and suffering can be diminished, or even eliminated, with a willing heart, some simple skills, and—most important—the courage to become a *peacemaker*.

BE THE PEACEMAKER IN YOUR HOME

While every couple should pray for peace, *peacemaking* involves taking action. It is the consistent readiness to reconcile mutual differences by seeking to listen to, honor, and learn from your spouse. Peace is the oil that makes the engine of your marriage run smoothly in spite of your differences, even during times of suffering. Peacemaking is the foundation for unity, which, in our view, is the key to lasting satisfaction, joy, and intimacy in marriage. But it doesn't just happen automatically. You and your spouse must each *strive* to be a peacemaker, seeking common ground and mutual benefit rather than becoming entrenched in your own agendas or selfish desires. As it says in Scripture, "Better a dry crust with peace and quiet than a house full of feasting, with strife" (Prov. 17:1).

Your marriage can *survive* if one of you takes on the role of peacemaker, but it will only *thrive* when you and your spouse each purpose to become a peacemaker. And this will require you to individually ask God to deal with the stubborn pride that inhabits the recesses of your hearts. You will need God's help to consistently confront your very human tendency to act on your natural motivations of selfishness and pride. Our flesh wants to protect itself. We recoil or lash out when we are hurt, disappointed, rejected, offended, disrespected, neglected, treated unjustly, or ignored. Scripture identifies the real root issues underlying arguments in marriage with laser-like accuracy:

> What causes quarrels and what causes fights among you? Is it not this, that your passions are at war within you? You desire and do not have, so you murder. You covet and cannot obtain, so you fight and quarrel. You do not have, because you do not ask. You ask and do not receive, because you ask wrongly, to spend it on your passions. (James 4:1–3 ESV)

The more prideful we are, the more we are being conformed into the image of Satan, the ultimate example of arrogance and selfishness. But the more we choose humility, the more we are being conformed into the image of Jesus, our ultimate example of humility and selflessness. Pastor Ronnie Bachelor taught me some key principles about peacemaking when I heard him officiate a wedding service. I encourage you to reflect on his insights and look for ways to apply them in your own marriage.

> Here's your commitment to one another: "When life is not a party, I will not leave you!" The test will be, can you exhibit covenant love when days are routine or disappointing or tough? This is certain: In your marriage, you will be sinned against. You will be offended. You will hurt each other's feelings. You will have moments of hurt, pain, and suffering. Will you, by God's grace, actively pursue your spouse's highest good in that moment? That will be the true strength of your marriage, the grace you exhibit toward each other's sin. . . . The love of Christ is our standard . . . our guide . . . Christ's love was a sacrificial, pursuing, intentional love. If you are to preserve the integrity of this truth, you must love *first*! You love *first*.

Peacemaking can be practiced in the following ways: being the first to apologize, choosing healing words, learning each other's love language, resolving misunderstandings and differences of opinion, and learning to treat each other as friends rather than enemies.

First to Apologize

One couple I have counseled came to see me for a meeting with a look of death about their marriage. This couple—let's call them Steven and Sarah—would not speak to each other or even cast a glance in the other's direction as they sat in my office. Some couples just look like they belong together, and they did. But there obviously had been significant challenges in their relationship after only six years of marriage. I prayed silently that the Lord would give me wisdom to help them. But the tension only increased when Sarah pulled me aside and shared that she was at the end of her rope.

I was taken aback by the futility in her words and felt the weight of her despair on my shoulders. Again, I silently asked God to help me as I looked up at Sarah. She stared back with seemingly empty eyes and I sensed her pain was truly more than she could continue to bear.

After setting a few ground rules—no interrupting or arguing—I began by asking each to take a turn explaining the problem in their marriage. To my surprise, neither of them revealed any terrible sins or secrets. They had both remained faithful and committed to their vows. They didn't seem to have issues with pornography, physical or verbal abuse, and there had been no financial disasters. In fact, they didn't seem to have any real money problems other than their continual arguments. But each of them recited what seemed to be a long and itemized list of disagreements and disappointments—times they had hurt the other. They both were very good at keeping records of wrong. Finally, I thought I recognized the underlying problem and began to speak to them.

"Satan has built a wall between the two of you. That wall is so tall that it feels like it reaches all the way to heaven. Neither one of you can scale it so you are each feeling hurt, lonely, and miserable. You are each stuck on your side of the wall."

They nodded in agreement. Obviously, I had said nothing that was not already abundantly obvious to both of them! I needed fresh insight. Praying, I searched for a way to help them. Prompted by the Holy Spirit, I asked another seemingly simple question: "When was the last time one of you apologized to your spouse?"

Sarah was the first to speak up. "Never. We have *never*

apologized to each other in all our years of marriage."

I was stunned but waited to hear Steven's reply.

"Sarah is right. Never. She does not apologize for her wrongs against me. I don't apologize for my wrongs against her."

Realizing the Holy Spirit had revealed the root issue in their marriage, I said, "Unless one of you is willing to be the first to apologize, your marriage will not be healed. God is a God of mercy, but repentance and forgiveness are central tenets of the gospel. He forgave us while we were yet sinners and we should be willing to forgive each other. One of you must be willing to humble yourself and apologize for the ways you have hurt your spouse."

This was the moment of truth. Neither of them moved and time seemed to stand still. I had no idea how long to sit in silence. It was so quiet I thought I could hear my watch ticking. My mind raced as I wondered whether to give up and when to end the counseling session.

Without warning, Steven made a sudden movement and I heard a strange noise. I could not immediately tell what was happening. He then pushed back his chair as if he were going to stand and leave, but with a lurch and a thud, he fell

> THE FIRST TO APOLOGIZE IS THE BRAVEST. THE FIRST TO FORGIVE IS THE STRONGEST. THE FIRST TO FORGET IS THE HAPPIEST. —Author Unknown

to his knees and burst into tears. As he wept aloud, he crawled across the gap between their chairs until he reached Sarah's side. He took her hands and pleaded, "Please forgive me! Please forgive me for hurting you. I am so sorry. I love you, Sarah. Will you forgive me?"

Sarah clasped her hand over her mouth in shock! Like me, she was startled by her husband's tears and apology. His words obviously struck a chord deep in her heart and tears began to pour down her face. Her expression of anguish was transformed into peace. I could tell healing was taking place. It was a holy moment. A beautiful expression of grace and mercy broke across her face as she exclaimed, "Yes! Yes! I forgive you! Will you forgive me? I love you too!"

Satan was defeated before our very eyes. Their pastor later told me, "If you had never seen a miracle before, then you sure have now." He was right. God saved a marriage and a life before our very eyes.

When Steven apologized despite his own heartbreak and anger, then asked for Sarah's forgiveness, it changed everything. Don't miss this. The moment when they both apologized and chose to make peace, healing began immediately. Here's why. Humility met a response of humility. Even though their differences were still great, both of their hearts had been opened to forgiveness and reconciliation.

Now can you see why I was so encouraged by Steven's willingness to apologize? He was brave. You should strive to always be first to apologize, first to forgive, and first to forget. Do not wait until your spouse deserves it. Do not wait until you have received an apology. Do not compile a history of your spouse's past mistakes to use against him or her in the future. You will only be digging a hole in which to bury your marriage.

Gentle, Healing Words

When you learn to act as a peacemaker in your relationship, Satan's attempts to destroy your marriage will be thwarted. When you and your spouse actively choose to make peace, forgiving each other for your mistakes, you safeguard your marriage against Satan's attacks. He cannot prevent you from experiencing the advantages of working together in unity unless you are unwilling to forgive each other; it is as simple as that.

From Proverbs we learn, "The wisest of women builds her house, but folly with her own hands tears it down" (14:1 ESV). The same sentiment applies to you too, husbands. Be ready at all times to extend grace to your spouse. Scripture is very clear in its call for us to be peacemakers. Husbands and wives should both take to heart the admonitions in the following verses.

It is better to live in a corner of the housetop than
in a house shared with a quarrelsome wife.
PROVERBS 21:9 ESV

As charcoal to hot embers and wood to fire,
so is a quarrelsome man for kindling strife.
PROVERBS 26:21 ESV

Continual conflict will begin to rapidly diminish when you learn to use gentle, healing words instead of verbally attacking and hurting each other. Remember this promise, "A gentle answer turns away wrath, but a harsh word stirs up anger" (Prov. 15:1). Ann and I have some ground rules for settling our conflicts that we have found helpful.

Don't:
- Call your spouse a derogatory name or label
- Use curse words
- Make threats
- Refuse to talk or engage in the conversation

Do:
- Remain calm and logical
- Choose to use helpful words
- Find common ground for agreement
- Seek to solve the problem

Remember, God has made two into one: that means when you hurt your spouse, you are simultaneously hurting yourself. "Harsh words" stir up anger and have the capacity for great harm. James makes this quite clear: "How great a forest is set ablaze by such a small fire! And the tongue is a fire, a world of unrighteousness. The tongue is set among our members, staining the whole body, setting on fire the entire course of life, and set on fire by hell" (3:5–6 ESV). And within the context of marriage, words have great power. Ann and I have seen the destruction of many marriages as a result of words being used as weapons. But this too can be undone. Words can be used as a healing balm.

In his letter to the Colossians, Paul gives us practical insight into the proper use of words: "Let your speech always be gracious, seasoned with salt, so that you may know how you ought to answer each person" (4:6 ESV). Kind words that are seasoned with salt preserve our relationship and point one another back to Christ. They build up instead of tear down. Proverbs provides a similar admonition on how to use words: "A gentle answer turns away wrath, but a harsh word stirs up anger. The tongue of the wise adorns knowledge, but the mouth of the fool gushes folly" (15:1–2). In the moments when you feel disrespected, unloved, overlooked, fearful, or angry, you can avoid conflict and instead of saying what first comes to mind, practice using words that restore, bring calm, and seek agreement. C. S. Lewis offers hope to all couples who find themselves caught in constant conflict: "Love in this second sense—love as distinct from 'being in love'—is not merely a feeling. It is a deep unity, maintained by the will and deliberately strengthened by habit."[6] He understood that, just as choosing to react negatively has become a habit, we can choose to love and make it a habit.

The impetuous disciple, Peter, gives us this practical advice: "Finally, all of you should be of one mind. Sympathize with each other. Love each other as brothers and sisters. Be tenderhearted, and keep a humble attitude" (1 Peter 3:8 NLT). This often boils down to a better choice of words, or as my former pastor, John Batusik, would often say, "You can easily improve your marriage today by eliminating three hurtful things you chose *not* to say."

LEARN HOW TO SHOW EACH OTHER LOVE

Dr. Gary Chapman has identified a common problem in marriage, which is a fundamental misunderstanding of how to communicate love to each other. In fact, most of us tend to communicate love to others in the way we prefer to receive love. But this tendency can lead to much conflict in marriage when each spouse is trying to communicate love but most likely in a way that does not connect. In order to be successful as a peacemaker, it will be critical for you to understand yourself and your spouse and, in particular, the ways in which you are made to feel loved. Ann and I highly recommend Gary's book *The 5 Love Languages*. Learning the primary way each of us receives love has made a tremendous difference in our relationship.

My love language is Words of Affirmation, so I feel most loved when Ann uses words that build me up. This was initially hard for her to comprehend. How could I possibly need more affirmation? Don't I receive enough validation already? Wouldn't her words of praise just inflate my ego? Surely I didn't need her to constantly say, "I love you," or "You are handsome," or "Great job!" My response? I told her I would prefer that she say something like, "I am crazy, passionately in love with you and can find no other man who is a tenth of the man you are!" Or she could say, "You are the most handsome man I have ever laid eyes on and you only improve with age!" Or even, "You were fantastic in the way you courageously, flawlessly handled that problem for me. I could not imagine anyone doing it better than you!" Those are the kinds of words that thrill me to my core and communicate Ann's great love for me.

I travel often for work and my travels frequently take me to faraway places. Oftentimes Ann cannot join me since she is maintaining our home and caring for our children. I always ask her to accompany me but she simply cannot always get away. On one recent trip, she wrote me a series of notes and hid them in my luggage. These were not silly notes but notes filled with authentic expressions of her love for me, her commitment to pray, and her support of my work. I found the first one tucked inside my blazer's side pocket just after I arrived at the airport. She knows that's where I tend to keep important items when I travel. I found the next note when I arrived and began to unpack my bags. Later, I found another inside my shaving kit. Then another was stuck inside my extra pair of shoes. Our boys wrote a few of the notes, and it was obvious she had given them all much thought.

These thoughtful notes blessed me to the core of my soul. The intentional words of affirmation gave me strength, courage, confidence, liberty, joy, satisfaction, and pleasure. Ann's loving words put a spark in my eyes, quickness in my step, and eased the pain of being away from home. I felt loved, fulfilled, energetic, and ready to do the work ahead on my trip.

However, Ann's primary love language is Acts of Service. That means she feels most loved when I do something that serves and supports her, things like sweeping out the garage, helping with the boys, keeping up with household maintenance, or raking the leaves. These are all actions that speak to Ann of my love for her. Honestly, I find this so foreign that I could not comprehend it until I read Dr. Chapman's book. Previously my tendency was to express my love in the way I preferred to receive it, telling Ann, "I love you. You are beautiful and you are a wonderful wife. You are an excellent cook. Great job with the housekeeping! You are the best mom in the entire world!" I fully expected her to be blessed and feel loved. Nope. She wants action. She feels loved when I step up and show her with my deeds.

I once heard a woman say that the most romantic words her husband could say to her were, "I've got it, honey." Whether it was a big thing or a little thing, he would respond, essentially, with, "I'm on it. Consider it done!" His Johnny-on-the-spot answer made her feel loved. Another friend of ours agrees: "When my husband does something I ask, and doesn't complain or drag his feet, it makes me feel cherished. But if he kind of blows it off . . . it really bothers me. I had to tell him, 'Look, this may not be that important to you. But it is to me. And that should be enough for you.'"

My wife doesn't want to argue about *why* she wants or needs something done. Rather, she desires that I exhibit a helpful attitude that shows my love and care for her. Obviously not every woman's love language is Acts of Service, but I do believe that we as husbands have a unique ability to demonstrate love to our wives by our actions.

It took me a while to appreciate the rewards of learning how to show one another love in strategic ways. But I have become convinced that God designed us to respond to each other more fully and sincerely when our emotional relationship is whole and strong. And our ability to effectively communicate love to one another is a key aspect of peacemaking. It is the surest way to increase intimacy and stimulate our romantic bond. Ann and I have to work at this. We are not perfect. But the fires have never gone out.

Cultivate Your Friendship

One husband that was seeking to put some of these principles into practice told me that following an argument, his wife once said, "I just wish you would treat me as good as you treat your friends. You are so kind and understanding with them. Everyone else seems to get your best behavior; I get what's left over. Why is that?" She stated this as an observation and a genuine area of concern, not an accusation. It stopped him dead in his tracks. He immediately knew she was right.

"That very day," he said, "I asked the Lord to help us become friends—best of friends, not just husband and wife trying to get along. I vowed to give her my best. It changed everything."

In early 2015, former president George H. W. Bush and his wife, Barbara, celebrated seventy years of marriage. And by all accounts, their marriage is a testament to the importance of being friends with your spouse. When asked about her marriage, Mrs. Bush has said: "I think we grew together. I think that when you have a child die and you survive, and you've been through a war and you survive, and you build a business and you survive, you either grow apart or together. We always turned to each other."[7]

The *New York Times* recently reported on a new study that shows "being married makes people happier and more satisfied with their lives than those who remain single—particularly during the most stressful periods." The study's authors say, "Marriage may be most important when . . . things are going wrong." Of course, I believe this boost to life satisfaction comes from being committed friends. The study finds that "those who consider their spouse or partner to be their best friend get about twice as much life satisfaction from marriage as others." This is especially true during middle age when life and family stresses are at their highest because "they have a shared load and shared friendship."[8]

Ann and I are continuing to learn how to relate to each other as best friends. We seek to give each other our best just as we would a dear friend who walked into our home asking for help.

PUTTING PEACEMAKING INTO PRACTICE

Conflict is a dangerous threat to your ability to align your finances and unite your hearts. Overcoming this threat will require vigilance and a strong commitment to being a peacemaker in your home. As we have learned, you cannot build on a foundation of conflict; you can only build on a foundation of peace. God wants your marriage to flourish, but that will begin only when you each surrender your desire to lash out, argue, and fight. When you surrender this, your heart will be conformed to God's image because He is a God of peace. Remember the words from Galatians: "For the entire law is fulfilled in keeping this one command: 'Love your neighbor as yourself.' If you bite and devour each other, watch out or you will be destroyed by each other" (5:14–15); and, "But the fruit of the Spirit is love, joy, peace, forbearance, kindness, goodness, faithfulness, gentleness and self-control. Against such things there is no law" (5:22–23).

Finally, I want to give you four practical tips to help you cultivate peace in your home, which you and your spouse can put into practice today.

Resolve Conflicts Promptly

Don't go to sleep with unresolved conflicts. Ann and I have made this our practice for years. The Bible makes it clear that resolving disagreements is our daily responsibility: "Do not let the sun go down while you are still angry, and do not give the devil a foothold" (Eph. 4:26–27). We should not postpone making peace after arguments or we put ourselves in danger. Satan is clearly looking to establish a pattern of discord to continuously erode your close relationship. Going to bed angry typically causes you to wake up with more energy to fight. And like a small stone in your shoe, if given enough time, the anger will cause a blister, which can become infected. And ultimately, this pattern will undermine your peacemaking efforts and jeopardize your relationship. Make things right with your spouse. Go apologize.

> LIKE A SMALL STONE IN YOUR SHOE, ANGER WILL, IF GIVEN ENOUGH TIME, CAUSE A "BLISTER" THAT WILL JEOPARDIZE YOUR RELATIONSHIP.

Learn from Your Mistakes

This is a critical practice within marriage. When you apologize to each other, make an effort to understand what went wrong in order to avoid repeating the same mistake. Pain is an effective teacher. Once experienced, we naturally try to avoid it in the future. It is like the warning light on the dashboard of a car, both helpful and instructive. When the red light comes on, the car is experiencing pain! The light is the indication that the driver must stop, inspect the problem, and take steps to fix it. The warning light helps avoid a total loss! So don't just dismiss the pain of conflict and hope it will go away. Rather, get to the real reason for the pain and work together to fix it.

Confess Your Error and Affirm Your Spouse

Go beyond an apology and acknowledge your spouse's wisdom. Begin by saying, "I am sorry. Will you please forgive me?" Then, add these important words: "I was wrong and you . . . you . . . were . . . right."

It can be hard for us to say these words. But now, go further and express what you learned. For example, "You were right. I should have taken care of the electric bill before it came due. That procrastination caused the power to be turned off, we lost fifty dollars in late penalties, and the food in the refrigerator is spoiled. I will pay the bills on time next time." While it may seem difficult, this extra step brings both healing and instruction by openly expressing your commitment to preventing the pain in the future. This is a very helpful practice for both men and women. You will be so encouraged by the progress you make following this advice.

Stop Quarreling

Make an effort to stop quarreling, even if you do not agree with your spouse or he or she is not a Christian. In 1 Peter 3, we receive clear instructions for both men and women, followed by an incredible promise. Don't miss this.

Wives, in the same way submit yourselves to your own husbands so that, if any of them do not believe the word, they may be won over without words by the behavior of their wives, when they see the purity and reverence of your lives. Your beauty should not come from outward adornment, such as elaborate hairstyles and the wearing of gold jewelry or fine clothes. Rather, it should be that of your inner self, the unfading beauty of a gentle and quiet spirit, which is of great worth in God's sight. (vv. 1–4)

Husbands, in the same way be considerate as you live with your wives, and treat them with respect as the weaker partner and as heirs with you of the gracious gift of life, so that nothing will hinder your prayers.

Finally, all of you, be like-minded, be sympathetic, love one another, be compassionate and humble. Do not repay evil with evil or insult with insult. On the contrary, repay evil with blessing, because to this you were called so that you may inherit a blessing. (vv. 7–9)

Now listen clearly to the promises to the husbands and wives who follow this practical advice.

For, "Whoever would love life and see good days must keep their tongue from evil and their lips from deceitful speech. They must turn from evil and do good; *they must seek peace and pursue it*. For the eyes of the Lord are on the righteous and his ears are attentive to their prayer, but the face of the Lord is against those who do evil." (vv. 10–12, emphasis added)

The Lord promises to listen to the prayers of the peacemaker! Commit to being a peacemaker. Quickly resolve arguments, fights, division, and discord. Don't go to bed angry with each other. Learn from your mistakes. Acknowledge your spouse's wisdom. Commit to becoming best friends. These practices will bring the fullness of God's shalom into your home and will be the cornerstone of preserving your unity as husband and wife. His Holy Spirit will give you the fruit of love, joy, and *peace*!

> Clothe yourselves, all of you, with humility toward one another, for "God opposes the proud but gives grace to the humble." Humble yourselves, therefore, under the mighty hand of God so that at the proper time he may exalt you, casting all your anxieties on him, because he cares for you. (1 Peter 5:5–7 ESV)

BE AT PEACE

We need to be personally experiencing the peace of God (Phil. 4:7) to have a supply of God's love when we are besieged by conflict. Be sure to spend time in prayer and reading the Scripture to prepare your own heart for the attacks that will surface. The more you are experiencing the peace of God, the more those around you will also experience it.

Hear the words of two leaders well acquainted with the search for peace amid conflict:

> "Peace is not absence of conflict, it is the ability to handle conflict by peaceful means."—Ronald Reagan
> "Peace is the beauty of life. It is sunshine. It is the smile of a child, the love of a mother, the joy of a father, the togetherness of a family. It is the advancement of man, the victory of a just cause, the triumph of truth."
> —Menachem Begin

As we close this chapter, let me note here that Ann and I have prepared some practical application resources to help you put the seven keys into practice. You'll find this material in chapter 9. It is important to complete these exercises to establish unity and create benchmarks for your progress. We have also written a pledge so that you and your spouse can commit to practicing each of these important building blocks for your alignment and unity. Feel free to complete the exercises now or after you have read all the chapters.

And now that you have committed to becoming a Peacemaker, let's move on to the next key: grasping the biblical definition of Prosperity. Without a biblical understanding of how God defines true prosperity, you will be battered by the fruitless chasing after all the false alternatives. This next key will give you hope of aligning your financial strategies at the same target and uniting your hearts under God's definition of what it means to flourish and prosper in your marriage.

CHAPTER TWO

Key #2: Grasp the Biblical Definition of Prosperity

"For I know the plans I have for you,"
declares the LORD, *"plans to prosper you and*
not to harm you, plans to give you hope and a future."

JEREMIAH 29:11

"WATCH OUT!"

Imagine those words being directed toward you by some-one you love. It should capture your attention immediately. Now imagine those words coming to you from Jesus Christ. "Watch out! Be on your guard against all kinds of greed; life does not consist in an abundance of possessions" (Luke 12:15). Our Lord gave us warning not to fall into the trap of material-ism. This silent, insidious sin has taken captives throughout history and, given the smallest opportunity, will wreak havoc in your marriage.

But what is materialism exactly? For many, materialism can be easily identified as the desire created by these five words: more, bigger, better, faster, newer. It is an attitude of discontentment and a greedy drive to have more stuff. It is a false philosophy of what it truly means to prosper and as such it divides couples and destroys lives. Jesus revealed the heart issue underlying the desires for more, bigger, better, faster, newer in this one word: greed.

Now, no one is eager to admit to his or her greed. Most think it is a problem that exclusively afflicts the rich. I have met very few people who say, "Wow, I am materialistic and need to change!" It is subtle, elusive, and very dangerous. So how do you know when *you* are at risk? Maybe this will help you identify it—materialism happens when our desires are activated by greed and destroy our contentment. It is a drive to gain *more*, believing that more (fill in the blank) is essential to your happiness. Marketers prey upon this drive by simply introducing a new smartphone with some better feature than the one you currently have, making you feel yours is subpar. It is what makes people stand in long lines waiting for a store to open to rush in to grab the stuff they want when Christmas sales season begins.

Although the Bible firmly warns us to beware of it, I (like so many) was generally ignorant of the dangers materialism posed. Further, I had no idea what the Bible said about what it means to "prosper." Wasn't it okay to be rich, and wasn't that an encouragement to be materialistic? Once I declared to Ann, "I dream that one day we will be rich. Maybe it will take a golf cart to get around our property." She was not impressed. At that time we were barely earning enough to afford our humble apartment. So I set out on the path, but silently. My secret desire was to prove through financial success that I could do anything I set my mind to. This hidden greed was rooted in my heart for the first twenty-one years of our marriage! It was not until I repented of my sin and renewed my mind on God's truth that I became free of materialism and learned God's view of prosperity.

Not only did the philosophy of more, more, more grip my

life, I have seen it happen to others I have encountered in my years of teaching and training. First Timothy 6:9 says that "those who want to get rich" can fall prey to all kinds of grievous sin.

REACHING FOR THE FIVE Cs IN SINGAPORE

The country of Singapore is considered an economic miracle. In just fifty years, this tiny island nation has gone from having nothing to becoming one of the richest nations in the world. One in every six residents is a millionaire. Although the costs of real estate, car ownership, and country club membership in Singapore are some of the highest in the world, these metrics gauge an individual's economic status. The "Five Cs"— standing for Cash, Credit Card, Condo, Car, and Country Club—are also known as the "Singapore Dreams," and they have become part of the culture of this nation.[1] You need to obtain all 5 Cs to be a really prosperous Singaporean. Having visited there many times now, I know that the 5 Cs are an empty and shallow definition of true prosperity.

As John Piper says in *Don't Waste Your Life*:

> I am wired by nature to love the same toys that the world loves. I start to fit in. I start to love what others love. I start to call earth "home." Before you know it, I am calling luxuries "needs" and using my money just the way unbelievers do. . . . I sink into a secular mindset that looks first to what man can do, not what God can do. It is a terrible sickness.[2]

This is a glimpse into how I operated early in our marriage. It did not bring peace to our relationship or our finances. The harder I worked, the more distant Ann and I became. I thought she wanted more money, even though she never said it or asked for it. She was content. I was discontent. She wanted more of me, not more money. The harder I worked chasing more, bigger, better, faster, nicer, the less I invested in the priorities of our home. There was no contentment in my heart and it affected our marriage.

Much like Singaporeans, most of us have an ideal or target for what it means to prosper. My definition of prosperity was to make millions of dollars: to get rich *in a hurry*. I came out of business school with a belief that the scorecard in business and life was based upon how much money I could earn. And of course, how much of that could be put on display by the things I was able to purchase. That was not even close to Ann's definition. She was cautious with money and wanted to focus on using it as a means to build our family and follow God's priorities for our life. Ann felt that I did not care about her values. It also made her worry about me and the financial decisions I made without her input. Ann would tell me that the family needed more of my focus at home, but I was driven by my ambition and ignored the warning signs.

Materialism had a grip on me. I brought this belief system into our marriage, effectively dividing us from having the same goal, thus rendering any joint planning futile. This became one of the greatest challenges for me personally; in fact, I was not able to transform my attitudes without God's intervention, which I will share more about in the Philosophy chapter.

I have given thousands of live presentations in my life, and I often cover the topic of materialism and its deadly consequences. At one of my recent talks, I was asked to give practical help and perspective to men whose lives were being controlled by excessive working hours, crushing pressures, and stressed-out families due to the high expectations to become successful. About two thousand men were scheduled to attend, and I was a little nervous about the message I planned to deliver.

For the next several hours, I taught my heart out about the real meaning of life, how prosperity is not the purpose of our life, and how we can so easily waste our lives pursuing the wrong goal. I pointed out how the messages in books such as the wildly popular *Rich Dad, Poor Dad* by Robert Kiyosaki contradict God's Word. I occasionally glanced at the expressions displayed by my audience to see if anyone was getting angry again or had gotten up and left, but all remained and seemed to be engaged in my talk.

> GETTING RICH SHOULD NOT BE OUR ULTIMATE GOAL IN LIFE.

When the event concluded, I made my way to the book table to greet attendees and sign copies of my books. I braced myself, expecting to get an earful of critical comments about my talk. But I was wrong. Instead, once I was seated behind the book table, a gentleman politely asked me to stand up. As soon as I stood, he leaned over and gave me a big hug and burst into tears. Swallowing hard, he said quietly, "Thank you. Thank you. Thank you."

This was a dramatic and unexpected turn of events. He went on to share his story with me, explaining that twenty years earlier he had moved to Singapore with the singular dream of getting rich. He also told me that he was a "disciple of Robert Kiyosaki" but that he had failed miserably in all his businesses and investments. And in his pursuit of wealth, he said he ruined his life, lost his family, and was now completely broke. His wife had divorced him and moved with their children back to their homeland. He now felt he had no reason to live. But that morning, a friend had encouraged him to come to the men's conference. Despite much inner conflict, he ultimately decided to board the public bus, place his last coins into the bus driver's hands, and show up to the event.

He closed his story by telling me I was the first Christian who explained that getting rich should not be our ultimate goal in life. He had never understood the biblical definition of prosperity and that materialism had led him down a path of destruction and despair. He shared that he was now set free and able to pursue God's design for prosperity.

Imagine the damage done to his wife, his children, and to himself all because of this wrong understanding of what it means to prosper. Unfortunately, his experience is not unique. Satan divides men and women at every economic stratum over this same issue. And this false teaching has crept into the church under the guise of the so-called "prosperity gospel." And it is so damaging to families and the body of Christ. We must recognize that it is Satan's tool, not God's. It is time that we understood prosperity from God's perspective before we expend our life's energy pursuing some personally defined goal or lifestyle that ultimately will not please God.

MORE THAN MONEY

Most of us have heard the Hebrew word *shalom*. It is understood around the world to mean *peace*. However, that is only one small part of its meaning. Shalom is more than simple peace; it is a concept that denotes completeness, wholeness, health, peace, welfare, safety, soundness, tranquility, prosperity, perfection, fullness, rest, harmony, and the absence of agitation or discord.

In modern Hebrew, the related word *shelem* means "to pay for," and *shulam* means "to be fully paid."

In Isaiah, Yeshua is referred to as *Sar shalom*, or Prince of Peace, which perfectly describes the ministry and personality of our Messiah (Isa. 9:6). Our God came to give us His *shalom*, a complete wholeness, fullness, and harmony, not simply a prosperity or peace based upon an abundance of money.

One of the verses most often cited on the topic of prospering is found in Jeremiah 29:11: "'For I know the plans I have for you,' declares the LORD, 'plans to prosper you and not to harm you, plans to give you hope and a future.'" I have seen far too many pastors and fellow believers claim this verse as their personal promise from God that they will have unlimited wealth and material prosperity. Unfortunately, they have completely missed the meaning behind this verse as well as the actual prosperity plan that God so generously gave to us in verses 5 through 10! It is important to note that the Lord gave these instructions to displaced people. The Israelites had *nothing* and were captives in a foreign land. This was God's plan to help them to start over and rebuild their lives from scratch. This was His blueprint for experiencing all the good He had planned for them. But it would require a change of heart and mind before they would actually agree with God and act upon it.

I encourage you to read this entire passage in Jeremiah 29:5–11, and then we'll go through this key to understanding God's prosperity plan step by step.

Step One: Get a Job and a Place to Live

Build houses and settle down;
plant gardens and eat what they produce.
JEREMIAH 29:5

Every society and family is built by individuals who take responsibility to establish an income and a place to live. This is the basis of stability and a foundation from which to build and grow. Without this, we see folks living like perpetual wandering tribesmen or migrant workers moving from job to job. It is very difficult if not impossible to build a marriage and a family without a place to live and a source of income. Prosperous lives are built upon stable foundations, and both income and housing are foundational.

The Lord's plan is that we each plant and eat from our own garden—that is, work to take care of our own needs. This clear directive has many contemporary social and cultural benefits. With the most basic of needs being met, this person will be able to direct his efforts and concerns beyond his and his family's own needs. In modern terms, this equates to establishing a consistent source of income. Paul's reminder in his second letter to the Thessalonian church supports this principle. He described a rule that had been established preventing those who were unwilling to work from partaking in charitable feeding programs (2 Thess. 3:10).

A healthy marriage must begin with two essential elements in order *to be settled*: a source of income and a place to live.

Step Two: Get Married and Start a Family

Marry and have sons and daughters; find wives
for your sons and give your daughters in marriage,
so that they too may have sons and daughters.
Increase in number there; do not decrease.
JEREMIAH 29:6

According to Jeremiah, once a place to live and a food supply (in our case, an income) have been established, a settler is ready for expansion. A spouse and children can now be added to the home. Don't miss this key point. God's advice is to get married and have a family! So God designed marriage as a key part of His plan for us to flourish! In our contemporary minds, this may be the most controversial step in God's prosperity plan, but marriage and children have been and will remain an essential part of God's design to bring prosperity to our lives. For more of my thoughts on this topic, see the appendix: A Case for Marriage and Families. Let me add, too, that God can and will bless those who are single and couples who are childless. The key point is that marriage is a means by which prosperity is increased, not decreased.

Embracing God's definition of prosperity must include advocates for growing healthy families who view themselves as stewards to manage and expand the resources they have been given. We want you to be among those who cherish their children as a source of God's prosperity plan. They are real and lasting treasures in life!

Step Three: Seek Prosperity for Others

Seek the peace and prosperity of the city to which
I have carried you into exile. Pray to the LORD for it,
because if it prospers, you too will prosper.
JEREMIAH 29:7

After securing a private dwelling, a personal food supply, marrying, and starting a family, it is essential to look outward and become focused on the needs of others. This step requires a commitment to 1) seek community peace first, because prosperity cannot be obtained unless there is peace—the two go hand in hand; 2) seek community prosperity, not just your own; and 3) pray to the Lord for the peace and prosperity of your entire community. The Lord gives an astounding principle here: couples must embrace God's plan to help *others* prosper because our personal prosperity is dependent upon the peace and prosperity of our community (our local economy).

Step Four: Unify Your Hearts

"Do not let the prophets and diviners among you deceive you. Do not listen to the dreams you encourage them to have. They are prophesying lies to you in my name. I have not sent them," declares the LORD.
JEREMIAH 29:8–9

The spiritual condition of you and your spouse impacts everything else. What we believe about God impacts our view of ourselves and thus our marriage, children, and finances. God wants our hearts turned fully to Him first and then He will bind our hearts together—putting this into action as you attend church together, pray together, read books that will help you grow in your faith, serve others together, and learn to spur each other on as brothers and sisters in Christ.

THE LAW OF INVERSE PROSPERITY

Economies are a collective enterprise made up of the contributions of the members of society in that home, community, state, and nation. We are independent in one sense because of private home ownership and responsibility for our personal food supply, but we are totally *inter*dependent when it comes to developing a flourishing economy.

God's plan makes it clear our ultimate call is to seek and bring about His *shalom* in our families and communities. Christians are to serve the needs of others through peaceful means rather than through domination, manipulation, coercion, or force. We must also help others prosper, seeking a win/win in all our endeavors with the clear goal that those we are serving have the priority of the first win! This is counterintuitive and turns modern capitalistic greed and aggression upside down. This also eliminates the selfishness threaded in the false teaching of the "prosperity gospel," also known as the "health and wealth gospel."

We are to build enterprises that will assist others in the achievement of their goals and objectives. This is the best marketplace strategy of all time and is a key for anyone desiring to improve his or her economic future. Not only will one have an enterprise that will likely succeed, it will have real market value and will bless others with its products and services. This is a profound business and development principle. It must be the attitude of the heart for all of us who desire to prosper. However, it requires an attitude and motive that can only be achieved by those with a heart and mind grounded in Christian truth.

Imagine being free of materialism and living content with what you have. Now imagine going to work tomorrow and asking for a private meeting with your boss. You walk in the room, shake hands, and say, "Today, I am here to help you prosper. That is my goal. Just let me know what I can do better to make sure that is happening." First, your boss might faint in disbelief. But after you prove your sincerity, he will likely grow to trust and appreciate you more and more. Over time, you will become a valuable member of his or her team.

Early in my career, I briefly sold real estate for a residential homebuilder. My boss, who owned the company, was a man of integrity with high standards of professionalism. In our interview, he told me that because I would be working on straight commission that he doubted that I would be able to succeed in the business. With few other options at that time, I asked him if he would give me a chance. By God's grace, the very first month on the job, I was able to make a large sale. My boss was surprised and very happy. This continued month after month. Before long, I was responsible for the majority of the revenue in his company. He was financially prospering, and so was I. We grew to deeply appreciate each other and the experience pointed out the truth in this principle that if we help others prosper, we will also prosper.

Greed, coveting, survival-of-the-fittest tactics, corruption, and constant stress will plague the heart and economic fortunes of any man or woman who only sees God as the responder to our personal demands to be made rich. God's true economic message is that we are to trust our needs will be met through our obedience to God's prosperity plan. We must demonstrate trust in His faithfulness to provide for our needs as we serve the needs of others. When couples align their hearts in this way, their own prosperity is entrusted to God's care.

Let me offer you hope if you are reading now and thinking to yourself, *My spouse and I will never get unified because we are not like-minded.* Ann prayed diligently for me for most of those years when I was in the snare of materialism. She endured the pain and frustration I caused by casting her cares upon the Lord. In a practical sense, we both suffered financially since we were not giving, saving, or investing with a unified goal, but she did not give up trusting that God could change me and unite our hearts. And He did!

We must embrace God's definition of prosperity and unite by living according to it. This will bring more than prosperity; it will bring *shalom* to your relationship as husband and wife and to your family.

Content, Not Complacent

To be free of materialism is to learn to be content. Paul described the state of contentment that is available to all whether we have abundant possessions or very few: "I know what it is to be in need, and I know what it is to have plenty. I have learned the secret of being content in any and every situation, whether well fed or hungry, whether living in plenty or in want" (Phil. 4:12). Paul expressed our unique privilege as believers of finding contentment in Christ, not in things. And his timely encouragement ended with these words, "I can do all this through him who gives me strength" (v. 13).

But let me caution you here. Learning to be content does not mean you become complacent, lazy, or unwilling to work to achieve good things for your family. We can be ambitious and successful in our endeavors while still trusting God and being used for His purposes. Ann never had to worry if I was going to work or seek to provide for our family. The key is to be unified on God's definition of

> LEARNING TO BE CONTENT DOES NOT MEAN YOU BECOME COMPLACENT, LAZY, OR UNWILLING TO WORK TO ACHIEVE GOOD THINGS FOR YOUR FAMILY.

prosperity so it is integrated into your joint values and does not prevent you from flourishing as a family. Complacency will lead to worry, stress, and lack. Contentment will lead to peace, unity, and fulfillment—both financially and spiritually.

Thingdom vs. Kingdom

Often, couples get very divided over where, how, and on what to apply their focus once materialism has rolled into their marriage. Several years ago, a friend told me of an experience in the small-group Bible study he was leading. It was made up primarily of young couples, all of whom had experienced significant financial success. In their first meeting as a group, the six couples were gathered in a living room and were asked to introduce themselves. Soon it came time for the Johnsons (not their real name) to share. They were a handsome couple, both in their early thirties. They had three young children. She worked part-time while her husband worked as a corporate attorney in a large multinational firm. They seemed to have plenty of money, a comfortable life, and a secure future. But after sharing briefly about themselves and their children, Mrs. Johnson said, "I am not sure why we were invited to be in this group. We are not as rich as the others here!" That drew a brief laugh. But she continued, "My husband and I work hard but I have figured out how we can catch up to the others in the group."

"Really?" she was asked politely. "Do you have a strategy to achieve that goal?" One could see her husband's face begin to turn red from embarrassment. Perhaps he knew what was coming and was hoping that she would keep the information private.

"Oh, sure I do!" she exclaimed with a big smile on her face. "Six lucky numbers. That is my strategy!" The group roared with laughter. But her husband shrank back in his seat. It was obvious they were not unified behind her plan! She went on to describe to the group how she purchased a lottery ticket *every week* and was praying for God to give them a windfall of riches so they could keep up with their circle of friends and have everything their hearts desired. Yep. She really said it.

I appreciated her honesty and transparency even though the leader reported that it made her husband cringe.

Jesus addressed those who were worried about life's basic necessities in Matthew 6. His reply is telling: "So do not worry, saying, 'What shall we eat?' or 'What shall we drink?' or 'What shall we wear?' For the pagans run after all these things, and your heavenly Father knows that you need them. But seek first his kingdom and his righteousness, and all these things will be given to you as well. Therefore do not worry about tomorrow, for tomorrow will worry about itself. Each day has enough trouble of its own" (Matt. 6:31–34). Our financial worries often lead us to seek first to build our own thingdom. Jesus said that should not be our focus. We are here on earth to build His kingdom. When we make that our top priority, He takes care of our needs one day at a time.

Back to our friend who was praying to pick winning lottery numbers. I learned that she and her husband successfully completed one of Crown's financial Bible studies together and at the end of the course, they were totally united. God brought them together and helped them identify a common goal for their family prosperity. Not only did she quit purchasing foolish lottery tickets, she came to see the wisdom of her husband's approach to their finances. They aligned their goals and united their hearts by establishing they would seek Him first in their lives.

BREAKING MATERIALISM'S GRIP

So how can we escape the grip of materialism? Here are a few ideas.

Examine your views of prosperity in light of Jeremiah 29:4–11.

Make giving your top priority. Anonymous giving is even better.

Giving consistently will break the grip materialism has on your heart.

Give away something that you deeply treasure.

Practice meekness in your lifestyle choices. Put far less on display than is held in reserve.

Get involved with serving the poor in your community, nation, and world.

Give of your time by volunteering to work on church and community projects.

Begin to pray together that your treasures will be in heaven and not on earth.

Examine where you are spending most of your time. Are your friends encouraging more materialism or less?

Limit your exposure to advertising, commercials, and shopping.

Read God's Word and biographies of heroes of the faith. Go on a short-term mission trip together.

Establish financial goals that impact God's kingdom instead of building your own "thingdom."

Write your obituary and include how you hope to be remembered.

Be grateful for all that God has provided that money cannot buy.

I encourage you and your spouse to complete the exercises in chapter 9 in order to reflect on and implement the material in this chapter. I have now covered the first two keys to aligning your finances and uniting your hearts. Next I will present the third key: Know and Fulfill Your Life Purpose. This next chapter will address the major division that hampers so many couples from making real progress toward accomplishing their financial goals and fulfilling God's purpose for their lives.

CHAPTER THREE

Key #3: Know and Fulfill Your Life Purpose

Many are the plans in the mind of a man,
but it is the purpose of the LORD that will stand.

PROVERBS 19:21 ESV

Work as hard as you can, to make as much
money as you can, to retire as early as you can,
to entertain yourself as long as you can.

MY PARAPHRASE OF THE AMERICAN DREAM

EARLY IN OUR marriage, the *work-make money-retire-play* strategy accurately summarized the purpose I had embraced by default. Ann and I fell into the category of couples who did not intentionally align on our life purpose. I *assumed* that the American Dream was a purpose Ann could agree with and get behind. While we both wanted children, we never really discussed our purpose as husband and wife or our purpose if God chose to give us a family. Thomas Merton once said, "People may spend their whole life climbing the ladder of success only to find, once they reach the top, that the ladder was leaning against the wrong wall." It can be even worse if the husband is climbing one ladder and the wife another.

In the previous chapter, we established the importance of grasping and adhering to God's definition of prosperity. This gives couples a common financial target and provides clarity as to what your labors are directed toward, saving you and your spouse the heartaches of materialism. It also helps to answer the *What* questions related to work, money, and marriage and define the outcomes you desire to achieve through your job and career. But we need more than a biblical understanding of prosperity. We also need a united answer to the question, *Why are we here?* You each need to know why God put you here on earth and what He wants to accomplish through you as husband and wife. You then become very intentional about achieving that common purpose. As David McAlvany states in his book *The Intentional Legacy*, "Intentionality begins with the self-conscious decision to wholeheartedly engage life. It proceeds with the recognition that your life is endowed with purpose."

When you haven't identified a clear life purpose directed by the Lord, both individually and as a couple, your hearts will be divided. With divided hearts, you will be prevented from developing a unified vision for what your life will ultimately count for or be used to achieve. Even worse, you are vulnerable that Satan will deceive you into taking on a task that fulfills his purpose.

A divine purpose answers the ultimate questions of: *Why am I here? What does God want me to accomplish? What does He desire for us to accomplish together?* Part of your responsibility as husband and wife is to look beyond the financial outcomes you aspire to achieve and on to how you hope to impact your family and the broader world you are called to serve. Purpose is intended to answer the big-picture questions about your lasting legacy.

I have found that many couples tend to make assumptions about their purpose. This is especially true when a couple falls in love and begins to dream about their future together as husband and wife. Oftentimes, they don't automatically or easily discover that they have vastly different ideas of what their real purpose in life is. One spouse may dream of a large family, living in an idyllic home, and having a "happily ever after" story. The other may have an unspoken dream of achieving something great outside the home through career or personal endeavors. This will inevitably lead to division and stress that pulls marriages apart. I am certainly not saying couples cannot have different interests, different careers, or different ideas of how to accomplish life goals. But I am saying they need to have a big-picture goal of what they are striving to achieve as a result of these collective efforts and especially their purpose as a husband and wife together.

GOD USES WILLING HEARTS: THE STORY OF NICK VUJICIC

Nick Vujicic had every right to be confused about the purpose of his life. Although he was born to godly parents with no history of drug use, medical problems, or genetic issues, and his mother's sonograms failed to reveal complications during the pregnancy, Nick was born with a rare congenital disorder that causes the limbs to be attached close to the trunk. In his case, he was born with no limbs whatsoever. As a child, Nick faced many challenges but he also struggled with depression and loneliness. Nick wondered often why he was different than all the other kids and questioned the purpose of his life, even contemplating suicide at one point.

I had the privilege of meeting Nick in person and interviewing him for my daily radio broadcast before he published his first book and became known around the world. We talked about his testimony and an encounter with Christ that completely turned his life around. At age fifteen, Nick read John 9 and the first few verses captivated his heart: "As he went along, he saw a man blind from birth. His disciples asked him, 'Rabbi, who sinned, this man or his parents, that he was born blind?' 'Neither this man nor his parents sinned,' said Jesus, 'but this happened so that the works of God might be displayed in him'" (John 9:1–3).

Nick explained in our interview, "I surrendered my life to Jesus after reading John 9. I knew I had to make my life right with Him but I had blamed Him for my pain. I read how Jesus said that the blind man was born that way *so that the works of God would be revealed through him*. I said to God that if He had a plan for that man, I certainly believed that He had one for me. I totally let go of 'needing to know the plan' and began to trust Him one day at a time." Nick told me he came to fully understand and accept the truth in Psalm 139: "For you created my inmost being; you knit me together in my mother's womb. I praise you because I am fearfully and wonderfully made; your works are wonderful, I know that full well" (vv. 13–14).

Since that time, Nick has become an ambassador for Jesus Christ, bringing hope and healing to the lost and hurting on every continent. Nick explains on his website that his purpose now is to help others find their true purpose: "Because of the ministry of Life Without Limbs, God has used me in countless schools, churches, prisons, orphanages, hospitals, stadiums and in face-to-face encounters with individuals, telling them how very precious they are to God. It is our greatest pleasure to assure people that God does have a plan for each and every life that is meaningful and purposeful, for God took my life, one that others might disregard as not having any significance and He has filled me with His purpose and showed me His plans to use me to move hearts and lives toward Him."[1]

He and his wife, Kanae, were married in 2012, and today they have two beautiful, healthy children. Together they are serving God's purposes as a Christ-centered family. Nick says, "If God can use a man without arms and legs to be His hands and feet, then He will certainly use any willing heart!"

Many Christians drift along through life, bouncing from one phase, event, or crisis to the next, guided by the tyranny of the urgent. The pressures and demands of paying the bills or keeping up with studies or meeting work goals or doing homework with the kids can prevent us from taking a serious evaluation of our life. This is especially true for couples. As Yogi Berra famously said, "If you don't know where you are going, you might end up someplace else." To stop this drift, we have to be intentional and disciplined about discerning God's purposes for our life.

THREE STEPS
TOWARD A UNIFIED PURPOSE

The Westminster Shorter Catechism begins with a question and answer that speaks to man's most pressing need to understanding his life purpose: "Question 1: What is the chief end of man? Answer: Man's chief end is to glorify God, and to enjoy him forever."[2]

Each of us, apart from our individual skills, talents, and gifts, have a common purpose to glorify God. And we should each seek to identify specific ways in which we can fulfill our personal calling while fulfilling our ultimate purpose on earth: to glorify God and enjoy Him forever. Once we agree that this is our ultimate, overarching purpose, many couples will begin asking how to determine a specific purpose as husband and wife. I will give you three steps to assist in this discovery process:

1. Know Thyself
2. The Sound-Mind Principle
3. The Trust and Obey Method

Know Thyself

We are each "fearfully and wonderfully made" (Ps. 139:14) and we are "God's masterpiece" (Eph. 2:10 NLT). We are made to fulfill His purposes, not our own. A helpful step toward that end is to know and understand our unique design and allow God to use us according to how He has made us. For instance, a John Deere tractor is designed to plow a field, but it would make for a very challenging ride commuting in highway traffic; likewise, a Honda Accord is designed to get you safely and efficiently around in traffic, but would be totally ineffective to plow a field.

In our case, Ann is designed by God to enjoy reading, studying, and learning. She is totally happy to curl up by a warm fire with a cup of coffee and dive into a good book. Given the choice between going to a movie and browsing through a bookstore, she will choose the bookstore or any opportunity to learn and grow every time. Although she is very capable of thriving in a variety of careers outside our home, Ann chose to use her gifts and talents to glorify God by educating our four sons. As of the writing of this book, she has been continuously involved in homeschooling one of our children for more than twenty-six years. She has operated within her design.

My unique design involves the gifts of leading, managing, and influencing. During the early years of our marriage, my career was in business. When God called me to serve in full-time ministry, there was a clear convergence of my gifts and talents that could be used to advance Crown's mission. If Crown needed someone to build houses, fix cars, program computers, or provide medical care, my gifts would not have been a good fit. My purpose, like yours, is to glorify God; my specific calling is serving in leadership at Crown.

As husband and wife, I support Ann in her calling, and she supports me in my calling. Together we are seeking to glorify God in our common responsibility of raising our family, homeschooling our children, and serving in my career as a ministry leader.

For those of you who don't know your unique design or how to discover it, I want to introduce you to a tool that can help. More than twenty years ago, Crown's founder, the late Larry Burkett, recognized that the first responsibility God gives us as stewards is to manage our gifts and talents. Larry went to work developing an assessment that helps individuals identify their gifts, talents, interests, and values. *Career Direct™* is a research-based tool that is one of very few psychological profiles that measures spiritual interests as well as other key attributes of our personalities. Beginning with a discovery of your God-given design, you can use the information gained from this assessment to help you understand each other's unique design. You will then be able to use this data to accurately seek how God can use your design to bring Him glory in all your endeavors.

The Sound-Mind Principle

Dr. Bill Bright, the founder of Campus Crusade for Christ (Cru), created a process that has been very helpful to me and to thousands of others. The process is taken from 2 Timothy 1:17: "God has not given us a spirit of fear, but of power and of love and of a sound mind" (NKJV). Dr. Bright called it "The Sound-Mind

Principle," referring to the distinction between a natural or carnal person who uses only common sense to make decisions, versus someone who is controlled by the Holy Spirit and has the advantage of God's wisdom and power when seeking His guidance. This approach provides freedom to make rational decisions based upon knowledge and wise counsel, while relying upon the Holy Spirit to control the final outcome.

Ann and I have found this approach to be helpful because it prevents us from being immobilized waiting on emotional or circumstantial or dramatic revelation to know God's will. Far too many of us are wasting our time and talents because we do not know God's plan for our lives. The process involves answering a series of questions and completing a few exercises as follows:

- What is the greatest thing you can do to help others?
- Make a list of the most logical ways through which your life can be used to accomplish the most for the glory of God with the desire to put His will above all else.
- List the pros and cons of each opportunity.
- Evaluate these opportunities in relation to your talents, training, personality, and other gifts God has given you.
- Ask yourself where or how, according to the Sound-Mind Principle, the Lord Jesus Christ can accomplish the most in continuing His great ministry of "seeking and saving the lost."[3]

Another filter I have added to this process is to ask myself, "Is Satan tempting me to do this?" Of course, if the answer is yes, I should not proceed. If the answer is no, it is likely that God is providing the inspiration for the desired action.

Dr. Bright always emphasized that this process can only be

valid if certain factors are present: you are not walking in obedience to sin, your life is fully surrendered to Christ, and you are filled and controlled by the Holy Spirit. It is also wise, in accordance with Scripture, that we seek the counsel of godly, mature Christians before finalizing our decision. This is the process I followed when Ann and I determined that God was calling us to leave the business world and serve at Crown. It provided us with assurance we were doing God's will and not our own.

The Trust and Obey Method

For many years, Psalm 37:4 has been a very important verse to me: "Take delight in the LORD, and he will give you the desires of your heart." I have taken the verse to have dual meaning. The primary meaning is that when we are focusing on God and delighting in serving Him, He instills new desires in us. We are transformed as God removes our greedy, selfish desires and gives us a genuine heart to serve others—and this desire springs from an overflow of God's unconditional love. This is the transformation that takes place by the renewing of our minds (Rom. 12:2).

But the secondary meaning I infer from this verse is a willingness by the Lord to assist us in achieving those things that our hearts appropriately desire.

When I was in college, my sister Cindy called me in tears to share her burden and prayer request. She did not finish high school, suffered from lack of control of her weight, and was painfully lonely. Her fear was that she was not meeting any men in the small community where we lived and would never be able to marry, which was the greatest desire in her life. Psalm 37:4 came to my mind. I asked her to surrender this desire to the Lord, to trust Him, to delight in Him instead of placing her hope in a future husband. I said it would be pleasing to God if her heart were content in Him, with or without a husband. I sensed she was not really trusting God but focusing on how she could provide for her own desires. We came to unity on this approach, prayed together, and waited on the Lord.

It was not long after that call that Cindy met the man that would become her husband. They were faithfully married and in love for almost forty years before she passed away. At her funeral, her husband played the audio recordings of the exchange of their wedding vows, declaring it to be the happiest day of his life. In my mind, I thought of God's faithfulness to Cindy. I thought of Psalm 37:4. I thought of the irony of trusting God and obeying His Word, even when we think He may not give us what we want or what is best; yet He does. God is always good.

Possibly you are like my sister Cindy, waiting on the Lord to provide the spouse you have long waited for. Perhaps you are painfully lonely right now. Possibly you and your spouse are deeply divided on your life purpose. Maybe one of you is not a Christian. Maybe you have considered divorce or separation; your marriage is in tatters. It may be that you are deeply divided over your finances and misaligned on how you want to operate as one. Let me assure you that God knows and cares about your pain.

I counsel you to trust Him fully. Obey His Word. Wait on Him to give you the desires of your heart. He may be working to change your desires. He may be at work to give you what you desire. Either way, it is important to delight in Him *today*. To fully surrender to Him today. To put your full confidence in Him regardless of your circumstances, your pain, or your heartache. I encourage you to record the desires of your heart here in the margin or somewhere you will see it regularly. Now write out Psalm 37:4 beside it. The Lord will take care of your desires as you find your joy fully in Him.

Ann prayed for unity in our marriage for many years. She longed to be united in mind and soul with me. She obeyed the Lord, waiting on me to also desire to obey Him. God answered her prayers. We now have a united purpose. Our hearts are united and our finances are aligned.

Once you and your spouse have established your common purpose to glorify God and have settled on your specific callings, you can unite your hearts to achieve these life goals and align your financial decisions to support them. Knowing your purpose as a couple will allow you to make decisions about where to live, what type of lifestyle you should have, and how to allocate your finances to ensure your purpose is achieved. A couple without a purpose is in danger of achieving nothing of eternal value.

SERVING THE LIGHT OF THE WORLD

Few couples have been a better example of making service to Christ the absolute purpose of their lives than Gertrude (Biddy) Hobbs and Oswald Chambers. When they saw the life-size version of the painting *The Light of the World* by William Holman Hunt at St. Paul's Cathedral in London, the pair were inspired by the call from Revelation 3: "Behold, I stand at the door, and knock: if any man hear my voice, and open the door, I will come in to him, and will sup with him, and he with me" (Rev. 3:20 KJV).[4] David McCasland said this in his book *Oswald Chambers: Abandoned to God*, "He and Biddy were pledging their love, first and foremost, to Jesus Christ, and to His work in this dark world. Their commitment went far beyond a hope for personal happiness to embrace a calling to belong first to God, and then to each other."[5]

Oswald and Biddy were married on May 25, 1910. When World War I broke out, Oswald wondered how he should serve his country. Sensing God's call, Oswald left his comfortable position in London in October 1915 so he could serve as chaplain to the troops in Egypt. Biddy and their young daughter, Kathleen, followed in December 1915. Biddy soon took up her ministry of hospitality and Oswald continued his teaching ministry to the troops. At first skeptical, the soldiers soon began to love and respect the Chambers family.

Tragically, Oswald died of complications following an operation to remove his appendix in 1917. The telegram that his wife sent home to family in England simply read: "Oswald, in His presence." His funeral paid tribute to a well-loved and respected man as did Biddy's chosen song at the funeral: "I to the Hills Will Lift Mine Eyes."[6] Mrs. Oswald Chambers now found herself widowed, alone, and penniless in Egypt, faced with the task of raising her young daughter. Many would have despaired in these circumstances but Biddy, who suffered from progressive hearing loss, had a special talent for lip reading and stenography. She had used her remarkable skills to capture the teachings of her husband each time he preached a sermon or delivered a devotional talk.[7]

During the months before Oswald's death, Biddy had transcribed his nightly talks from the book of Job and then she sent them on to the Nile Mission Press. The resulting book, *Baffled to Fight Better*, appeared in late 1917 and was quickly in demand in England, among soldiers and friends alike. Each month thereafter, Biddy sent one of Oswald's talks in pamphlet form to soldiers in Egypt and France. From this work emerged her sense that God's calling for her was to give Oswald's words to the world. When the last soldiers left Cairo in July 1919, Biddy and six-year-old Kathleen returned to England. With the encouragement and support of friends, Biddy began what she would always call "the work of the books."

From shorthand notes of Oswald's classes, sermons, and lectures taken during their short seven and a half years of marriage, she began publishing pamphlets and booklets, which were later combined into books. *My Utmost for His Highest* was first published in 1927, and has remained continuously in print ever since. Millions of people have been blessed and challenged by regularly reading this daily devotional. It has become one of the bestselling Christian devotionals of all time. Biddy died in 1966, knowing that she had fulfilled the purpose that God had entrusted to her and her husband.[8]

"FIND OUT WHO YOU ARE AND THEN BE YOURSELF"

Gaining alignment in your life purpose brings clarity, focus, and joy. It will move you from being distracted or disinterested stewards to being excited and fully engaged in the work God created you to accomplish. Without purpose, without a unified vision, your marriage will languish. Time and money will be wasted and joy will be sacrificed. And while God may not have called you to write the bestselling devotional of all time or to give all of your resources to advance His kingdom, He has called you and your spouse to give your utmost for His highest glory.

It is not my place to prescribe the focus of your life, that is, your purpose. But I do know for certain that it is never too late to be the "willing heart" that Nick Vujicic describes—a person who will allow God to be glorified through you. The Lord is actually looking for you now: "For the eyes of the LORD range throughout the earth to strengthen those whose hearts are fully committed to him" (2 Chron. 16:9). Ask the Lord why He put you on planet Earth. Commit this request to continual prayer.

The Crown Career Direct assessment can also be very helpful (available at http://www.careerdirectonline.org/). Larry Burkett always taught that our first responsibility as a steward is to manage our personal gifts and talents. He was fond of saying, "Each of us is as unique as a snowflake. Find out who you are and then be yourself." The unique Career Direct assessment provides accurate insight into your personality, skills, interests, and values. It helps you to understand how God has made you. With this knowledge of your real identity, it can be used to fulfill your true destiny.

Second, use the Sound-Mind Principle developed by Dr. Bill Bright. Surround yourself with godly counselors, arm yourself with the facts, and fully rely upon God as you make a rational decision about God's will. And finally, follow the Trust and Obey pattern to discern God's purpose for your life. Fast. Pray. If needed, seek help from godly, mature Christians to help you discern your unique gifts and talents and ultimate purpose.

It took me twenty-one years to fully surrender to the Lord's purposes. I wanted to be in charge and thus was primarily focused on self-fulfillment, not on a greater life purpose. When I finally acknowledged God's ownership and sovereign control over my life, it changed my entire perspective: my goals, my dreams, my ambitions, and our purpose as a couple. Ann and I were finally able to be unified. Our purpose today, our hope and dream, is twofold. One, that the Lord would use our children and grandchildren to bring Him glory, and two, that He would be pleased to use us to leave more faithful stewards on earth after we have departed this life than before we came. We seek to be good and faithful stewards of all that God has given us and to help others do the same. We believe our greatest purpose is to invest our lives first in our own family and then to the world beyond as we strive to hear those longed-for words of Jesus, "Well done, thou good and faithful servant."

Now, once your purpose is clear, being unified in your *beliefs* about money will create the alignment you need to make great spiritual and financial progress. To that we turn in the next chapter.

CHAPTER FOUR

Key #4: Live by God's Philosophy of Money

See to it that no one takes you captive by
philosophy and empty deceit, according to human
tradition, according to the elemental spirits
of the world, and not according to Christ.

COLOSSIANS 2:8 ESV

"MR. BENTLEY, I would like to set up an appointment to come and see you." The caller sounded intense, determined. He continued, "I need some help with my finances."

I was surprised, though perhaps *shocked* would be a better description. The individual calling my mobile phone was very well known; I would put him in the category of a celebrity. But I was not starstruck so much as dumbstruck as to why he would be calling me! Surely he had earned millions throughout his storied and celebrated career.

"Uh . . . sure," I said. "I'm happy to meet with you but before we set the appointment, I would just like to ask a few questions, if you don't mind."

"Not a problem. Go right ahead. But I can probably guess what you are going to ask me," he said.

"Okay. Very nice to meet you. Now, why do you need to see *me*? What is the issue that *I* can help you with?"

"Well, Mr. Bentley, I went to my pastor with this problem and he told me I needed to see a specialist like you, someone who knows how to deal with folks who have a financial problem like mine."

I was confident the pastor had mistaken me for a tax advisor and that I would soon be referring this wealthy person to a certified specialist who could help him with his taxes or estate planning. "Okay. What is it that your pastor thought I could help you with? Do you have a tax or estate problem?" I asked.

"No, no, no!" he said. "My problem may not be an actual *financial* problem." As he began to open up and speak freely, I sensed that he was in a great deal of pain. "I am so confused right now. I just need somebody I can talk to. The issue is that I recently got married and my wife and I cannot agree on *anything* to do with money. She likes to spend; I like to save. She thinks we are far richer than we really are. We argue and fight about money and I don't think I can take it much longer. She wears me out . . . but I really don't want a divorce. I want to make it work. Right now I feel I can't live with her . . . or without her."

I could hear the desperation in his voice, and I knew he was hurting on many levels. After a few more minutes of dialogue, the picture became clear: his young marriage was in deep trouble, he was in emotional turmoil, and he felt trapped in a lose-lose situation. If he remained married, his wife would spend so much money that they would soon be broke and become another celebrity boom-to-bust story. But if he went through a painful and publicly humiliating divorce, he feared he would end up losing so much that he could never recover.

With a slight break in his voice, he said, "I love her. I want this to work. I am just out of ideas on *how* to make it work."

I could relate to this perfect example of the hidden deception that divides two people with different philosophies of money, based upon their personal preferences. It was similar to my own experience and opened the door for me to share the journey the Lord took Ann and me on to become united.

Like him, Ann and I had been married for twenty-one years but found it difficult to agree about money. We had arguments, ongoing stress, and made financial mistakes brought about by wrong *philosophies*. Our challenge was that I did not agree with Ann and she did not agree with me. We loved each other, but a wrong philosophy about money was the key area of dysfunction in our relationship. We had two very different sets of beliefs about money. Until we were able to see where our *beliefs* were different, we could not agree on how to *behave* with money.

Ann thought *I* had a financial problem. I thought *she* had a problem because she did not agree with *me*. We were in a stalemate. We could not make any progress because we were never unified. She thought I was blind to my own foolish ideas and stubborn because I did not accept hers. She was right, but I would not admit it. My wrong philosophy was creating relational and financial problems because I had been deceived into thinking I knew everything I needed to know about money.

For many years, my wife prayed that we would become like-minded. In our relationship, I was the spender and she was the saver. She was more like this wise celebrity, worried about our future if I did not come to my senses. Ann asked me to join a Crown Bible study at our church on the topic of money. I thought that was the *last* thing in the world I needed to do with *my* time. It sounded boring and beneath me. But she persisted, and by God's grace, we found ourselves in this study, praying and memorizing Scripture together on money and finances.

During the study, it was revealed to me that I had held on to my own *philosophy* of money. For many, many years my beliefs did not agree with God's Word. This study helped me to see my error and to repent of my attitudes and beliefs about money. At that time, Ann gently asked me, "Do you agree with *God's* teaching on money?" I said, "Yes. I agree with God." She then said, "Good! If you agree with *God*, then I can agree with *you*!" That is how we finally became unified. It was the turning point of our marriage. We went from two competing philosophies to unifying under the one philosophy I had been ignorant of— God's. It even led me to write my first book, *The Root of Riches: What If Everything You Believe About Money Is Wrong.*

Reflecting on my own journey, I decided that the best course of action would be for me to send the celebrity the same materials that had helped us overcome our differences about money. Although I sent the materials, I never heard from him again and that was fifteen years ago. With a little search on the web, I learned he and his wife are still married and apparently have never gone broke! I am trusting the Lord that what I sent him was helpful!

One of the helpful discoveries God gave me regarding His plans for unifying couples was the insight that we are full of thoughts, ideas, plans, dreams, concepts, beliefs, and principles that together make up our *philosophy*. Philosophy was a subject I never cared much about in school since I thought it was for professors who liked to ponder the meaning of meaningless matters. That was before I experienced so much pain from my own faulty philosophy and observed similar pain in the lives of those I counseled.

For the first time, I understood that knowing God's philosophy of money is critically important since it protects us against the storms caused by deception. Satan started his attacks on marriages beginning with Adam and Eve and he has never stopped. He tries to deceive all of us with false beliefs about money. As Paul makes clear in his letter to the Colossians, the enemy uses human philosophies and empty deceit to lead us astray (2:8).

Whether we realize it or not, we all have diverse beliefs, both good and bad, and those collective beliefs constitute our philosophy. Further, those beliefs are the basis, or the root, of all our actions. We are designed by God to act upon what we *believe*, even when we are deceived and believe the wrong things! Therefore, our beliefs constitute the explanation for our behaviors, and in order to transform behavior we must begin by understanding what we believe, or our philosophy.

Over the years, I have encountered many couples whose philosophies about money were as different as night and day, and yet they had never identified or discussed those differing beliefs. Although they may have adopted different methods or techniques for managing their money, few couples get to the root issue of examining their core beliefs. This was true in my own marriage.

My first year of serving in ministry with Crown was an eye-opening experience. I had naively thought that financial problems were *behavior* problems and thus solved by a change of that behavior. Counseling session after counseling session dispelled my wrong view as I came to recognize how the underlying problems were actually caused by wrong *beliefs* that created chasms as wide as the Grand Canyon.

> RESEARCH INDICATES THAT THERE IS VERY LITTLE DIFFERENCE IN HOW CHRISTIANS AND NON-CHRISTIANS MANAGE MONEY.

WHAT DO YOU
BELIEVE ABOUT MONEY?

According to a recent article in *USA Today*, Americans report that the most common financial problems they face are:

- Making ends meet (35%)
- No retirement savings (31%)
- Too much debt (41%)
- Poor purchasing or investment decisions (38%)
- Unable to enjoy their money (10%)[1]

While this data did not include a survey of Christians, research indicates there is very little difference in how Christians and non-Christians manage money. But I have a surprise for you: none of the above financial problems are the *real* issue. Rather, they are all the fruit of underlying faulty beliefs about making ends meet, retirement savings, debt, investments, and enjoying money.

Whether you ask someone on the street or in the pew, a pastor, or a married couple, about their financial problems, you will likely hear all of them express their financial pain in terms of their behaviors. Our tendency is to only focus on our behaviors when we address our financial challenges. The hidden financial problem in your marriage is not how you *behave* with money; it is what you *believe* about money. Stated another way, it is not your financial condition that is the problem; it is the *financial lie* that leads to that condition. The lie is the root causing the fruit.

This problem of misdiagnosis is so prevalent that it is making financial slaves out of the body of Christ and keeping marriages in perpetual discord. This division occurs because a misdiagnosis always leads to mistreatment. We naturally make wrong decisions about how to solve problems if we don't accurately define the problem. If we think a patient has a cold instead of malaria, we might prescribe a bowl of chicken soup to make him well. All the while, he is in danger of death. He remains a captive to the disease.

Likewise, if I think I have a debt problem, I will seek to change my behavior to get out of debt. If I think I have a savings problem, I will seek a solution to increase my savings. Although getting out of debt or increasing our savings or creating a financial plan are admirable behavioral changes, and there is nothing wrong with those actions, our wrong beliefs are left unchallenged.

We have allowed beliefs to go unchanged and tried to fix the resulting problems through behavior modification. In many ways, we approach financial management in the same ways we would use to teach a chicken to play the piano. We point out what keys the chicken is to peck, then reward the good behavior with a treat. But here is the danger of leaving bad beliefs unchanged: beliefs determine our actions, which determine our direction and ultimately our very destiny.

All of us likely use a form of transportation that consumes gasoline or petrol as fuel. Imagine if I told you that all you had to do was to put water in the fuel tank to keep the engine running. If you did this, you would ruin your engine and make a costly mistake. But my guess is that you are saying right now, "That is ridiculous! I would never put water in my car or motorbike!"

Okay . . . but *why* would you refuse to put water in the tank? Is it not a cheaper, more easily obtainable liquid than gasoline? You say, "Yes, but it does not work!" Ah, I see. You do not *believe* water will cause your car to operate. You believe only gasoline will cause it to operate. That is my point about philosophy; it is the driving force behind our beliefs and leads to our behavior. As Craig Hickman states in *The Oz Principle*, "In fact, beliefs as a determiner of actions will trump action plans, reorganizations, new processes and systems, and the latest behavior-modification programs seven days a week. Yes, beliefs really are that important."[2]

Most financial training is focused on telling people what to do without supporting the behavior with the reasons why. So deception will stubbornly taint our thinking until the root issue is properly addressed. To experience lasting change, we must be convinced in our inner being, in our hearts and minds, to embrace the truth of a new belief, then to act upon it to change our behaviors. We see this truth throughout Scripture as well: "Above all else, guard your heart, for everything you do flows from it" (Prov. 4:23).

God's Word teaches us that we are changed into something brand new, transformed like a caterpillar becoming a butterfly, by a change in our beliefs. As it states in Romans 12, "Do not be conformed to this world, but be transformed *by the renewal of your mind*, that by testing you may discern what is the will of God, what is good and acceptable and perfect" (v. 2 ESV, emphasis added). Certainly we can be trained to change our behaviors. Elephants are subdued into obedience by ankle chains; monkeys can be trained with food rewards to perform tricks. But we are not elephants, monkeys, butterflies, or chickens. People can change their methods, plans, and techniques with money, but their real need is to be *trans*formed. And, "now that you *know* these things, you will be blessed if you *do* them" (John 13:17, emphasis added).

My desire is to see God's people free and marriages united, strong, and thriving, but in order for this to happen we must become *unconformed* to what the world has taught us about finances and have our minds renewed by God's truth. This does not occur with new behaviors but with a new set of beliefs.

Without this core shift in beliefs, we have only changed temporary outcomes, and financial problems will persist.

BELIEFS = BEHAVIOR

Thomas Cranmer, the father of Anglicanism and author of the first Book of Common Prayer, once said, "What the heart loves, the mind chooses and the will justifies." So the plumb line for truth is God's Word and the principles He gave us for our well-being. The Bible compares people to trees: "No good tree bears bad fruit, nor does a bad tree bear good fruit. Each tree is recognized by its own fruit. People do not pick figs from thornbushes, or grapes from briers. A good man brings good things out of the good stored up in his heart, and an evil man brings evil things out of the evil stored up in his heart. For the mouth speaks what the heart is full of" (Luke 6:43–45).

Good beliefs produce good behavior. When our root systems are transformed, our beliefs are unified and the fruit we produce as husband and wife will bless each other and the world. It is helpful for couples to look beyond the bad fruit that may present itself as rudeness, arrogance, stubbornness, pride, jealousy, out-of-control spending, envy, lying, cheating, stealing, unfaithfulness, and even debt as an issue of wrong beliefs. These behaviors are signs that a transformation of the heart and mind is needed.

Several years ago, I developed a simple technology to measure the beliefs and behaviors of Christians in nine key areas related to biblical financial management. I wanted something much deeper and more helpful than a credit score, which simply evaluates the likeliness of future debt repayment by looking at past behavior. The MoneyLife Indicator™ is a free assessment that helps individuals, couples, and organizations gain insight about their financial beliefs and financial behaviors (available at https://mli.crown.org/).

This unique instrument helps people understand what they truly believe and how they behave with regard to nine stewardship areas found in Scripture. The assessment consists of fifty-two questions and typically takes twenty to twenty-five minutes to complete. After completing the assessment, a detailed report is provided that also includes an action plan based on the three lowest scores for both beliefs and behaviors. Lasting change comes when we first modify what we believe. Once our beliefs are transformed, our behaviors will follow.

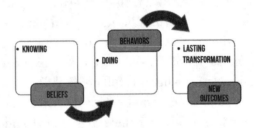

I highly recommend that you and your spouse use the MoneyLife Indicator™ to determine the areas where your beliefs disagree with God's Word and with one another.

This simple tool can assist you in assessing your attitudes and actions in nine key areas of biblical financial management: giving, work, saving, investing, planning, managing, debt, true riches, and legacy. The tool also includes recommended solutions for the areas where you need the most help. It is more important than your credit score. Both the husband and wife or boyfriend and girlfriend should take the assessment and compare your outcomes. If you find you have very differing beliefs, don't panic! Continue working through this book. As soon as you have finished this book, circle back to your MLI assessment and follow the next steps outlined in the report that you will receive. It takes some time and study of God's Word to become like-minded. But He will be faithful to make two into one!

"STUFF IS MEANINGLESS": COMING UP WITH YOUR OWN FINANCIAL PHILOSOPHY

The world is overflowing with an abundance of fine-sounding philosophies of money that are biblically inaccurate. Andrew Carnegie, the wealthy American industrialist, famously stated his philosophy of money: "The way to get rich is to put all of your eggs in one basket, and then watch that basket." This of course contradicts Solomon's principle of diversification found in Ecclesiastes 11:2: "Give a portion to seven, or even to eight, for you know not what disaster may happen on earth" (ESV). Once you recognize that you have been living based on faulty beliefs, the next step is to formulate a philosophy statement of your own that aligns with biblical principles.

One way to begin this process is to watch for and collect quotes that express a great biblical philosophy of money. These will help you to formulate a philosophy statement of your own. Here are a few good examples. In *The Cost of Discipleship*, Dietrich Bonhoeffer stated his financial views like this: "Earthly goods are given to be used, not to be collected . . . Hoarding is idolatry." Likewise, Pastor Paul Chappell has a concise financial philosophy that I appreciate: "God does not need your money; He wants what it represents—you. Finances are God's gift to you to fulfill His will for your life. While God desires you to prioritize His work in giving, He wants you to purpose to follow and serve Him no matter what happens with your finances."[3]

A number of our friends have developed simple philosophy statements that agree with God's Word and help them to unify around money decisions. Jess and Angela Correll of Stanford, Kentucky, summarize their philosophy in these four short lines:

> "Debt is bad.
> "Savings is good.
> "Giving is fun!
> "Stuff is meaningless."[4]

OUR PHILOSOPHY OF MONEY

Ann and I express our philosophy on money using a few simple principles derived from God's Word. These are the philosophies we believe and strive to live by.

Giving is the highest and best use of money (Acts 20:35).

Save consistently to be prepared for emergencies (Prov. 6:6).

Avoid hoarding (Luke 16:25).

Spending is an indication of where our heart is (Matt. 6:21).

True riches are more important than worldly wealth (Luke 16:11).

Debt is to be avoided (Prov. 22:7).

Investing requires counsel and caution (Prov. 12:15).

Imagine how much easier it is to talk about money when you're united around such statements of beliefs. For example, in the area of giving, our stated philosophy empowers each of us to be open and sensitive to God's leading on where and how to give. When the offering plate is passed at church, neither of us will be digging in our purse or wallet looking for loose change. We have a plan and a method of giving, which we enjoy. In fact, we set aside a sum of money every week for giving to our church, just as Paul advised the Corinthians to do. Instead of arguing about whether or not to give, our discussions revolve around how to give more, not less. We no longer experience tension about what we believe is the right financial decision. Instead we focus our efforts on how to best put those beliefs into practice:

- We seek each other's counsel and advice before investing or making major financial decisions. This has been a great source of protection and blessing to us.
- We tithe. Giving is an act of worship to us. We write a check and put it in the offering plate each week that we attend church. We are intentional about honoring those who teach us God's Word and help us grow as followers of Christ.
- We give to support the poor, advance the Great Commission, and respond to personal needs. A number of times we have given anonymously to individuals in need through our church. We practice Matthew 6:2–4.
- We seek to be frugal. We buy used cars, shop for second-hand clothes at thrift stores, and try to avoid paying full price for things we want or need.

- When we buy a new item of clothing or shoes, we donate something in our closet to avoid hoarding stuff.
- We delay gratification by being slow to make a major purchase. I start looking for a used car about a year before I will buy anything to be sure I know the market and am getting a quality vehicle at the right price.
- We have savings that would cover fifteen months of lost income and keep it aside for emergencies. This is a major accomplishment that takes time. Start small and be persistent. Don't give up. Three to six months of savings is essential, but for others fifteen months is better. Beyond that, money should be invested.
- We will joyfully spend money to invest in experiences, education, and programs that benefit our children or grandchildren. They are one of the banks where our true riches are stored.
- We match what our children save while they are at home. This has given us great joy and surprised the children when we ultimately transfer the funds to them as adults.
- The only debt we have is on the remaining balance to our home mortgage. We are working to eliminate that while also seeking to increase our giving each year.
- We diversify our investments and seek to have multiple income streams. Solomon spoke directly to both of these practices in Ecclesiastes 11:2 and 11:6. I recommend that couples operate by these two practices, as you are able.

In chapter 9 we have included a practical exercise to help you discover and develop your financial philosophy based on Scripture. It is a vital step to overcoming the deception that Satan uses to wreak havoc on marriages, so be sure to invest the necessary time to complete this. It will reward you with many hours saved from arguments and stress. The cornerstone of your financial plans must be built upon solid biblical principles—lest you build your financial house on sand.

In the next chapter we will discuss the importance of acceptance to avoid the devastation of rejection. Understanding and respecting your spouse's personality is—surprisingly—key to this process of unity.

CHAPTER FIVE

Key #5: Understand and Respect Your Spouse's Personality

Stop being mean, bad-tempered, and angry.
Quarreling, harsh words, and dislike of others
should have no place in your lives. Instead,
be kind to each other, tenderhearted,
forgiving one another, just as God has
forgiven you because you belong to Christ.

EPHESIANS 4:31–32 TLB

MY UNDERGRADUATE degree was in Business Administration from Baylor University. Unfortunately, accounting classes were required to graduate. And I don't mind admitting that accounting was difficult for me. One factor was my weakness related to advanced finance equations; but the other issue was that I was much more concerned with extracurricular activities on campus than studying. But in spite of my challenges in that first accounting class, it changed my life forever. You see, I met my wife, Ann, in Accounting 101.

I was sitting in the back row of the classroom with several

fraternity brothers when Ann entered the room. In addition to being beautiful, Ann is also very smart. She enrolled in pre-med at Baylor and was on an academic scholarship in the honors program. She eventually lost interest in medicine and changed her major to business. That's how God orchestrated our introduction in accounting. There she met me, her complete opposite! The very first evidence of this came in that accounting class when we made opposite grades on the first exam. She made a 95. And, you guessed it . . . reverse her grade and you'll know mine . . . I made a 59!

Of course, Ann's brilliance made me even more attracted to her. It was also God's providential leading that I was in the back row with my friends, since several of them began to discuss the possibility of asking her out. Before I revealed my intentions to them, I quickly asked her if I could give her a ride home after class. I didn't give the other guys a chance! Six weeks later I asked Ann to marry me and within ten months of walking into accounting class, we were married. My friends still tease me that I married Ann so I could pass accounting!

In spite of our love and commitment to each other, it did not take long to discover that God created us to be two *very* different people. To encourage you, *yes, to encourage you,* I am going to share some of our great personality differences, but don't assume that we were not "compatible." Personality is in part our God-given design and in part how we naturally respond to our environment.

For instance, I am an extrovert while Ann is an introvert. I like people—all people—everybody I meet! The more the merrier. Ann prefers to have deeper relationships with a few friends. This doesn't at first sound like a big deal, but I remember one of the very first parties we ever attended as a married couple. I wanted to arrive early and be the last to leave! Parties energize me! Fiesta time! Ann wanted to arrive late and leave early. Big parties can be overwhelming for her. I wanted to take her around to meet everybody. She wanted me to sit with her and stop walking around so much!

I like to talk. Ann likes to think. Talking is fun for me. When we have a problem, I naturally want to talk about it. Ann prefers to think about it. She wants to be left alone to process. Although she understands that the silent treatment is a punishment for me, when I interfere with her processing time, she asks me to "be quiet and think." She wants time to think and recommends that I do the same! I respond, "I can talk and think at the same time!" and "You should try it, you would really like it."

I am a big-picture person while Ann worries about the details. I am always thinking of exciting visions, dreams, opportunities, ideas, and creative ways to do something BIG! I am bored by details. Ann is cautious and wants to know the steps and detailed plans for how something is going to successfully take place.

At times in the past, I might blurt out to Ann (thinking it would sound romantic) that we should buy a boat and sail around the world together or something along those lines. I mean, why not escape the boring responsibilities of real life? Mostly it was just a daydream to temporarily take my mind off the day-to-day stress I was feeling at the time. Of course, I had not thought it through, I was just thinking out loud (remember the key point above about our differences). When I asked her what she thought, thinking to myself that surely she could not imagine anything more romantic than to be out sailing with me enjoying warm sunshine, ocean breezes, gorgeous sunsets, fruit drinks with little umbrellas on top, hopping from island to island with no cares in the world, Ann listened politely and then asked, "Do you have a plan?"

I responded, "Of course, I have a plan!"

She said, "What is it? How much will the boat cost? How long will we be gone? What time of year do you plan to leave? Do we need to sell or rent the house? How will you learn to sail? Who will feed the pets?"

I said, "Okay, okay, okay! Those are just details! It will all work out. Trust me! I have a plan! I don't know what it is yet . . . but I have a plan!"

Talking about my dream was just a way to escape current reality for a moment, and it went up in smoke as soon as Ann began asking about the *details*. She had to learn early in our marriage that I would suggest things I didn't intend to actually do. I had to learn that I need to think, think, think before talking, talking, talking!

As you can see, Ann and I are about as opposite in our personalities as a pit bull and a poodle. I have a Texas friend who once told me that I have "a personality as strong as cat food." You get the picture of the challenges Ann had on her hands from the beginning.

And this is not unusual, which of course can be very discouraging and stressful for both partners in a marriage. As I said earlier, don't be quick to jump to conclusions that "we are not compatible." That is a very different matter than having different personalities. But unfortunately, for a long time, I had the attitude that the personality God gave me was the *right one* and Ann's was the *wrong one*. She knew I felt she needed to be more like me for me to accept her personality. I know, it is painful to even admit it but I thank God that He gave her the strength and grace to endure as we worked through the challenges this caused. The ugly, subtle rejection was present and we desperately needed Jesus to bring us together. He has done that and will do it for you.

360° MARRIAGE:
WHY YOU NEED EACH OTHER

Couples often don't realize just how different they are until they are married. They have to begin making decisions together, especially when it comes to daily financial decisions. When you are dating, you have separate cars, closets, and bank accounts. The stress is much lower because, for the most part, decisions don't have to be made together other than where you want to have dinner. Once you are engaged, decisions must be made on just about everything regarding the wedding, the honeymoon, as well as the establishment of your home. After the honeymoon, even more decisions have to be made like whose brand of toothpaste will be the family choice? Even the smallest of issues can become divisive. Early on, our differences caused lots of misunderstandings, friction, and a sense of fatigue due to the constant reality that we view the world from very different perspectives. Our differences become even more evident when children arrive.

Ann's natural response to the world is 180° opposite of my natural response to the world. One day, about twenty years into our marriage, it occurred to me that this was not a liability or a problem or a mistake that needed to be undone or fixed. Rather, it was God's sovereign plan to bring together two very opposite people and make them one because each of us was *incomplete* without the other. We were perfectly designed to *complement* each other. My eyes were opened to the reality that I needed an opposite of me!

God knew I needed an introvert to place some boundaries around my extroversion; I needed a thinker to temper my desire to talk; I needed a detailed person to bring reality to some of my hopes and dreams that would never be achieved without a plan; I needed help to perceive the risks and dangers ahead; I needed a compassionate, sensitive person to help me learn to filter my words and think about the impact on the person that I was addressing; I needed a mate who would balance my desire to give spontaneously without regard for the future and to help me save and make progress in providing for the needs of our family. I realized without a shadow of a doubt that I would be a mess without Ann! She was exactly, without one deviation from perfect, what God knew would be needed to make me a whole man. Without her, I would be incomplete.

And God knew Ann needed a fearless extrovert to go out and make things happen, to meet new people and create new opportunities for our family. She needed a husband eager and willing to talk to resolve our differences instead of retreating into his own thoughts. She needed a husband willing to share his dreams and ambitions that she could help shape and improve upon. She needed a husband who would lead, take risks, and dare to do what God called us to attempt together. She needed a man who would complete her and complement the areas where she was not gifted.

Imagine two people standing back to back. They don't see the world the same way. Now imagine the two of them interlocking their arms. This simple gesture unifies two into one entity. When they begin to rotate, with one now looking to the east and the other to the west, they have a complete view of the world. They have become a 360° couple. They literally "have each other's back" and can protect and strengthen one another. Crown's late founder, Larry Burkett, was fond of saying, "In marriage, if both of you are the same, then one of you is not necessary." Regardless of our differences, the Lord wants us to love and honor our spouses.

Research confirms the benefits of being a 360° couple. Take

for instance this study published in 2014, which examined the impact of five key personality traits on career effectiveness and in particular looked at the working spouse's success when their partner displayed high levels of conscientiousness. When one spouse is conscientious—sometimes called "picky"—it has a positive impact on the other spouse's job, promotions, and income.[1] In an article about the study published in *Harvard Business Review*, Andrew O'Connell noted that "researchers found that the only spousal trait that was important to an employee's work outcomes was conscientiousness, which turns out to predict employee income, number of promotions, and job satisfaction, regardless of gender."[2]

Isn't that fascinating? Obviously, I believe that God intentionally orchestrates marriage as a way for spouses to be strengthened and helped by being united to someone with very different abilities. This is why opposites attract! This was confirmed by one of the authors of the original study: "When you're in a relationship, you're no longer just two individuals; you're this entity. . . . The more solid the entity, the greater your advantage."[3]

Can you say Amen for the blessings of your spouse? God gave that very distinct personality to help you, not to harm you! Let's work through this a little more deeply.

DOES PERSONALITY MATTER IN MARRIAGE?

Conventional wisdom tells us that opposites attract. I would add to that phrase my own personal modifier: after opposites attract and get married, they will then attack. Although Hollywood scripts, novels, music, and poetry are replete with romanticized stories of unlikely pairs finding each other irresistible, the phrase likely has its origin in the field of magnetism. When you hold two magnets close to each other, the two ends that repel each other have the same pole, either positive or negative. But when you put opposite poles together, they attract—hence the phrase "opposites attract."

But psychologists and relationship experts report conflicted findings on this issue. Personality is simply one dimension of who we are as people. We are also made up of skills, interests, values, talents, family backgrounds, and personal habits. We can have happy marriages whether we are married to a complete opposite or someone with an identical personality or any degree in between. Scientific research confirms this, even among non-Christians.

A recent study on the elements that contribute to a happy marriage found that compatibility is less important than previously thought. According to an article reflecting on this study's findings, "neither personality similarities nor differences appeared to affect how happy the couples were. The findings suggest the personality matching carried out by dating websites may make little difference in a relationship's ultimate success."[4] So be careful not to make too much of each other's personality. More important than personality is submission to God; both spouses need to be conformed into His image, bearing the fruit of the Spirit. When two opposite personalities are each submitting to God and His truth, character traits like flexibility, forgiveness, adaptability, compromise, kindness, and support will flow from each other. Listen to this advice from Paul very carefully:

> Put on then, as God's chosen ones, holy and beloved, compassionate hearts, kindness, humility, meekness, and patience, bearing with one another and, if one has a complaint against another, forgiving each other; as

the Lord has forgiven you, so you also must forgive. And above all these put on love, which binds everything together in perfect harmony. (Col. 3:12–14 ESV)

The transformational power of God's Word provides an advantage for two to become one regardless of your personalities, background, past mistakes, or annoying habits. Ruth Bell Graham put the practicality of this truth this way, "A happy marriage is the union of two good forgivers."

Study Your Spouse's Personality

There are many wonderful tools to help you know and understand each other's personality. I recommend that you make use of one or more of these personality profiles for your spouse. Become a student of each other. Know and understand how God uniquely created you and your spouse. Celebrate the Master's workmanship in creating your "other half." The two of you have become one. We know this by how much it hurts us when we hurt our spouse and how much joy we have when our spouse has joy.

To assist you in putting this important key into action, we have some practical exercises for you to work through in chapter 9. Now it is time to look at the final two keys, where we will cover the issue of building a Plan and following a Process. These will help you align not just your beliefs . . . but your behaviors as well.

CHAPTER SIX

Key #6: Create a Unified Financial Plan

Commit your work to the LORD,
and your plans will be established.

PROVERBS 16:3 ESV

The plans of the diligent lead surely to abundance,
but everyone who is hasty comes only to poverty.

PROVERBS 21:5 ESV

ARE YOU CONFUSED about money? Many are. One couple I counseled explained to me that they were "debt free." When I asked about how this good news came about, the wife explained that she had transferred all of their credit-card debt from seven cards to just one card and they did not have to make a payment for one full year. She was confused, to say the least.

Another couple I worked with felt they were too broke to live on a budget. They had been broke for more than five years, often not having enough cash to put gas in the car to get to work. They liked buying lottery tickets every week but resisted establishing a plan to live within their means. They were both confused about what it means to make a financial plan and the freedom it could bring to their lives.

Approximately 70 percent of the couples I have spoken with are living by "default," not by "design." Those who resist living by design are perpetually struggling because they do not have a plan. Financial plans are often thought of as unimportant early in life. Couples tend to think that love and sunshine will get the bills paid. But reality sets in the moment the rent is due, the car needs new tires, and the utility bills are higher than expected. Without a plan, and with no foundation for building unity as a couple, confusion can lead the most loving of couples into a nightmare of trouble and pain.

We have been carefully building a foundation of what some call the "soft issues"—those factors that most of us mistakenly assume have little bearing on the practical aspects of managing money. The truth is that the soft issues are often the more difficult ones to manage. These are human issues, not just the cold, hard numbers. Before you begin to build your plan, you should understand the following: what it means to be a peace-maker; God's view of prosperity; how to establish a common life purpose; how to align around a God-centered philosophy of money; and how to honor and respect each other's personality. You have done some important foundational work and are now ready to build a plan, and not just a financial plan but one that will unify your entire marriage.

As you establish this financial plan, our hope is that you don't simply create a plan to get your head above water. Rather, my hope is that this plan will help you go wherever God is trying to take you and your family. We want you to dream about a plan that will fulfill your life purpose and align with biblical values of prosperity. But let me warn you now, no matter how much you plan, Satan will work overtime to keep you from planning, and if that doesn't work, he'll try to make the planning process a discouraging failure, and finally, he'll try to keep you from following the plan you've established. Ann and I, even today, have to work to eliminate the confusion that our enemy seeks to inject into the things we hope to achieve. Confusion can be prevented with a plan and two people who are united to keep the plan working.

RUSS AND KANDY: DIGGING OUT

Russ and Kandy Hildebrandt's story is so encouraging that it made them famous. I first heard about their remarkable journey out of overwhelming debt when their story became one of the top personal finance stories of the year in 2010. In just four and a half years, they paid back $123,000 in debt, which was more than twice Russ's salary of $60,000 a year.[1]

Russ, who was a quiet, diligent man and a chemist, had not seemed like himself lately. Or at least that was the first clue that alerted Kandy to a possible problem. Russ had seemed sullen, frustrated, and discouraged, and that was not like him. They would have described themselves as a typical middle-class American family, living in Wisconsin and raising twin girls about to become teenagers, and life was good. So Kandy could not figure out why Russ was not acting like himself and she became worried.[2]

Kandy did a little research and soon began to suspect that Russ had debt he was not telling her about. When she asked about it, he confessed that through the years, whenever they fell a little behind, he would borrow money to keep them afloat. He had maxed out a number of credit cards and even borrowed money from family members. But he didn't tell Kandy because he wanted to avoid worrying her. But these small incremental charges continued to grow until their debt was out of control. When Kandy found out, she did not get angry or condemn her husband. She was shocked to hear the amount they owed and it frightened her. But she was also relieved to know the source of the problem. Her faith seemed to kick in immediately.[3] Kandy acted right away as the Peacemaker even though she was the one who could have taken offense. She also helped them to divide roles and responsibilities, and because of their love and acceptance for each other and their common foundation of faith in Christ, they were able to unite quickly.

Their plan included many drastic measures. They first went to a not-for-profit agency to establish a debt management plan.[4] This was *after* two Christian financial planners advised them to file bankruptcy. They ruled that option out, believing since they had borrowed the money that they should pay it all back. Russ took on a second job working the night shift as a janitor at a grocery store in addition to his regular full-time work. He slept in the car for four nights a week to keep up with the grueling demands of holding down both jobs even through the harsh winters of Wisconsin. Kandy cut their family expenses in half, determining they would no longer go out to eat, could make do with home haircuts, and instituting strict grocery shopping lists. They even declined purchasing each other Christmas gifts. Both girls chipped in to do their part by earning extra money and finding ways to save money. All their extra income went toward the singular goal of paying back all their debt.[5]

Here's what is so remarkable. They continued to tithe a full 10 percent of their income throughout this journey and they also had a third child in the middle of working their plan. Now, fortunately not everyone finds themselves in such extreme financial difficulties. Hopefully you are not just now learning that your spouse has hidden massive debt from you, or that your household debts are twice the size of your annual income! Your challenges may be more of the everyday, "too much month at the end of our money" variety. Or maybe you feel pretty financially secure. Good for you! But you still need a plan.

THE ESSENTIALS

Whether you are facing overwhelming amounts of debt, struggling to make ends meet, frustrated over your lack of progress in achieving your financial goals, or trust has been broken, there is hope if you and your spouse will unify and make a plan. Be like Russ and Kandy. They made a plan together and took corrective action immediately.

Stop fighting, blaming, arguing, criticizing, or rationalizing the issue. Accept that you both contributed to the problem and take responsibility for solving it. Next, make a plan that you can follow. Don't try to wish the problem away. Don't wait on a miracle. Use your mind and hands to get to work. Do what you have to do to make progress. Most importantly, invite God into your pain. Ask Him for the strength, patience, and diligence to follow through on your plan. Give your plan a higher purpose like Russ and Kandy, who wanted to "prove God's faithfulness."

The first step in establishing your plan should be thirty days of carefully recording your spending so you know where your money has been going. Once this is completed, you are ready to set up a detailed monthly budget, including all of your monthly expenses and debt (mortgage payments, car payments, student loans, credit cards and store accounts, money owed family and friends). You can download a free budget form at crown.org (https://planner.crown.org/Default.aspx).

Ultimately, a budget is a guideline to help you spend less than you earn each month. This simple objective must be an essential part of your plan. When you are spending less than you earn, you can begin to direct your resources to the places needed to accomplish your financial goals, whether that is paying off debt, saving for retirement, or financing your children's educations. If you continue overspending, you will remain stuck in a cycle of debt and stress and financial confusion. Essential components of every financial plan should begin with these basics:

Work. Establish an income that will allow you to support your family and achieve your goals. Ideally you will be able to earn more than you spend each month. Additional jobs or sources of income may be necessary to ensure that you are earning more than you are spending. Ecclesiastes 11:6 says, "Sow your seed in the morning, and at evening let your hands not be idle, for you do not know which will succeed, whether this or that, or whether both will do equally well." Consider a home-based business based upon your skill or talents. I have a friend who has an adult son with a disability. She is not able to leave him alone. She started a fulfillment service that processes orders for small, Internet-based companies, all from the convenience of her home basement. It is an excellent, flexible part-time job and provides good income for their family. I also recommend *Love Your Work*, the newest book by Crown's president, Robert Dickie III.

Give. Commit to honor the Lord first. Proverbs 3:9–10 says, "Honor the LORD with your wealth, with the firstfruits of all your crops; then your barns will be filled to overflowing, and your vats will brim over with new wine." Since God owns 100 percent of all that you have and He has faithfully provided for you, I recommend that you make a commitment to begin giving 10 percent of your income to honor Him. Make Him first in your financial plans.

Save. After your income is established and you have maximized your talents in your calling and career, and giving has become a top priority, it is important to begin to save. Joseph saved in preparation for the great famine in Egypt. God says to consider the ant and become wise by also learning to save. Saving money each month will reduce your stress immediately. It is an essential habit to develop before you begin paying down debt. This will give you an Emergency Savings Account to break your dependency on credit-card debt in the future.

A WAY TO GET THERE

Once these essentials are in place, you are ready to make a complete plan. Years ago, I helped develop a simple tool to assist folks in making progress toward their financial goals. It is called the Crown Money Map and you can access it here: http://www.crownmoneymap.org/moneymap/Home.aspx. On one side of the map you can record your life purpose. Then, you make note of your short- and long-term goals and record your progress on specific steps to make your plan a reality.

The three key stages of your financial plan should be to Get Well, Do Well, and Finish Well. These stages are broken down into seven destinations on the Crown Money Map, which will get you on the path to achieving your goals and fulfilling your life purpose.

Get Well

Destination 1: Build Emergency Savings—Save $1,000

Destination 2: Pay Off Credit-Card Debts—We recommend using the snowball method. A debt snowball calculator is available at https://engage.crown.org/debt-calculator/.

Destination 3: Pay Off Any Consumer Debt—Increase savings and giving

Do Well

Destination 4: Adjust Your Plan—Save for major purchases, increase emergency savings

Destination 5: Save for the Future—Increase savings and giving

Destination 6: Invest Wisely—Buy an affordable home Begin long-term investing

Finish Well

Destination 7: Leave a Legacy—Invest your life and resources for God's purposes.

Crown has a *Money Map Companion Guide* that was developed to provide in-depth help for accomplishing each step of the seven Money Map Destinations. We also have an extensive library of free articles on a wide range of financial topics to help you accomplish your financial goals.

"STEADY PLODDING"

Now, there are many biblical and practical tips I can give you about planning. The Bible talks extensively about it. Consider God's warning that planning is a sure way to avoid ridicule:

"Suppose one of you wants to build a tower. Won't you first sit down and estimate the cost to see if you have enough money to complete it? For if you lay the foundation and are not able to finish it, everyone who sees it will ridicule you, saying, 'This person began to build and wasn't able to finish'" (Luke 14:28–30). Notice that God expects us to plan, while trusting Him with our future and understanding that He alone will bring it about: "The heart of man plans his way, but the LORD establishes his steps" (Prov. 16:9 ESV).

A friend of mine was fond of saying, "Failure to plan is planning to fail," which of course is a restatement of one of Ben Franklin's famous quotes. I don't want you to miss this vital step because it is one of the critical issues when it comes to dealing with money. Also make sure you or your spouse is in charge of your plan details, because making progress will require diligence and faithfulness.

Discipline is a behavior or action. It is the opposite of sloth and recklessness. God's Word speaks to the rewards of discipline: "No discipline seems pleasant at the time, but painful. Later on, however, it produces a harvest of righteousness and peace for those who have been trained by it" (Heb. 12:11). If you lack discipline, pick one area of your life and commit to being very disciplined about that issue for at least ninety days. Since it only takes approximately twenty days in order to develop a new habit, you will be well on your way to real progress.

I once challenged a friend to drink only water (no coffee, tea, or soda) for one full year in order to be more disciplined and improve his health. He did it. But little did I know that it also convinced him he could be disciplined with money as well! It was the motivation he needed to overcome years of telling himself the lie that he was "not a disciplined person." If you are very disciplined in one area of your life, you can learn to be disciplined in other areas; but if you are not disciplined in at least one area, you will struggle to be disciplined in any.

If you struggle with financial discipline, I suggest you start with one simple goal that you will commit to accomplish. Make it something achievable, like saving five hundred dollars in the next six months. Then repeat that goal or set another one. As it says in Proverbs: "Steady plodding brings prosperity; hasty speculation brings poverty" (21:5 TLB). Discipline requires that you take small, diligent steps toward your goals.

The other character quality needed to fulfill your plan is faithfulness. The Bible makes it clear that as God's stewards we are called to continual faithfulness, not success: "Moreover, it is required of stewards that they be found faithful" (1 Cor. 4:2 ESV). And faithfulness is measured in our heart and is a response to our belief in our faithful Provider, Jesus Christ. When we place our trust fully in Him, we are expressing confidence in His principles and His ways. God wants us to fully rely upon Him. There is no such thing as being partially faithful. You either are or you are not. On the day we stand before the Lord, we will not be asked if we were financially successful, but whether or not we were faithful to God. If so, we will be rewarded.

> THERE IS NO SUCH THING AS BEING PARTIALLY FAITHFUL.

The gospel of Luke explains that we are to be faithful to God in managing the smallest of our financial decisions and this is backed with a promise of true riches: "One who is faithful in a very little is also faithful in much, and one who is dishonest in a very little is also dishonest in much. If then you have not been faithful in the unrighteous wealth, who will entrust to you the true riches?" (Luke 16:10–11 ESV).

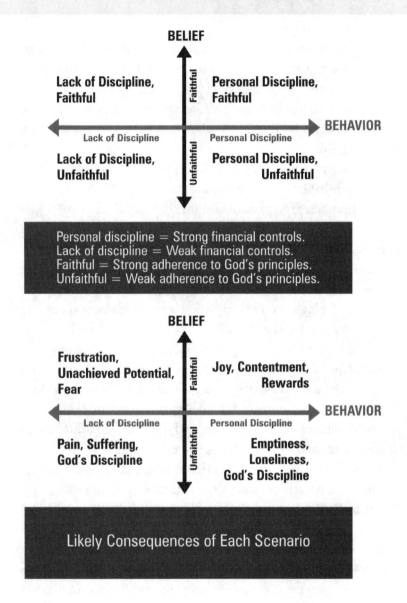

BELIEF

| Lack of Discipline, Faithful | *Faithful* | Personal Discipline, Faithful |

BEHAVIOR

Lack of Discipline | Personal Discipline

| Lack of Discipline, Unfaithful | *Unfaithful* | Personal Discipline, Unfaithful |

Personal discipline = Strong financial controls.
Lack of discipline = Weak financial controls.
Faithful = Strong adherence to God's principles.
Unfaithful = Weak adherence to God's principles.

BELIEF

| Frustration, Unachieved Potential, Fear | *Faithful* | Joy, Contentment, Rewards |

BEHAVIOR

Lack of Discipline | Personal Discipline

| Pain, Suffering, God's Discipline | *Unfaithful* | Emptiness, Loneliness, God's Discipline |

Likely Consequences of Each Scenario

WHERE DO YOU FIT?

Use the chart above to do a self-evaluation of the area where you tend to operate when it comes to your financial plans. Possibly you fall into the top left quadrant because you have a great heart for trusting and obeying the Lord but lack discipline when it comes to your financial controls. Maybe you fall into the lower right quadrant because you have lots of discipline when it comes to your finances but your heart is not submissive to the Lord.

It is important for you and your spouse to identify where you each believe you fall on this chart. It will help you know how best to serve each other. The goal is for the two of you to combine your efforts to move into the top right quadrant to be faithful and disciplined in your financial plans. It is also important to consider the likely consequences for each of these scenarios. The second chart will identify the likely challenges you are facing now and help you to know where you need to grow to ensure you are fulfilling God's plans for your life.

There is nothing wrong with rewarding yourself for improvements in this area. In fact, I believe God designed us to respond to rewards, so I encourage you to include small celebrations along the way as you gradually fulfill your plan. Matthew 6 illustrates how God holds out His rewards for those who are faithful. As an old pastor used to say, "What is rewarded is repeated."

Now take the time to work out your plan. Work through your plan together. Be sure to visit crown.org and utilize our free budgeting and calculator tools, as well as the Crown Money Map. Ask a godly mentor to hold you accountable if you need that extra motivation. I have found that most people quit following their plan due to a lack of progress, which creates discouragement. But you are on your way to freedom! Don't stop now. I encourage you to go now to chapter 9 for additional study and application tools.

And when discouragement comes—what should you do? Read on.

CHAPTER SEVEN

Key #7: Establish a Process That Ensures Success

*May he grant you your heart's
desire and fulfill all your plans!*

Psalm 20:4 esv

*But everything should be done
in a fitting and orderly way.*

1 Corinthians 14:40

HAVE YOU EVER felt like that hamster running around and around and around on the wheel? It is using lots of energy but making no progress in getting out of the cage! It can be that way when we're making sincere efforts to improve our money situation. We feel like we really are doing all we can do, but we're still not getting anywhere. Often I have observed that couples make plans, start strong, and then run into a roadblock and become discouraged.

Part of the problem is the unpredictability of financial circumstances. Maybe you have begun to save a little money and then the car breaks down, the hot water heater needs to be replaced, and one of the children has to go to the doctor . . .

all in the same month or week or day! Suddenly the progress you made setting aside some money in savings is gone, and you find yourself back to living from day to day or month to month.

Another trick of Satan is to discourage us by dividing us as a couple, making us question our unity. Maybe you have made progress in learning to work together, but another argument flares up and you sense you are back to where you started. Possibly you begin to feel hopeless and defeated; your confidence is shattered and you are worried about your ability to ever make it work following a major argument. (The worst are those Sunday-morning arguments—you know, the ones you have on the way to church. Ann and I don't argue *in* church, but we have certainly had our share before and after church!)

Discouragement is a powerful deterrent and should be recognized as an attack from the enemy of your soul. It can pop up over a single incident or from a series of painful events that rob us of the will to press forward in faith.

So what will help when we feel our spirits flagging? It's important to develop *processes* that keep your plan moving forward, even when a setback occurs. Like a well-trained emergency medical responder, it is essential to know what to do and be able to do it under pressure. Victory is attainable when you've been trained to keep taking that next action—in spite of how you may feel at the moment.

AN ARMANI SUIT AND A LESSON LEARNED

Ann and I have instituted a simple process that we call "Red Light, Yellow Light, Green Light." She was often discouraged by my unwillingness to listen to her counsel. We began to realize that when either of us became frustrated or discouraged, we lost focus on our plans and failed to make progress. This not only threatened our unity but our financial progress as well, even with a good plan in place.

Here's how it works. A red light means, "No. I do not agree with that decision." Yellow stands for, "Maybe, but not right now." And a green light indicates, "Yes. I can fully support that decision." Each of us gets a vote on any particular financial decision and it takes two green lights to move forward. If one of us responds with a red light, that means we are not going to do it. And we agreed there would be no more arguments or debates about it. If one of us votes with a yellow light that means we have to wait, pray, talk about it some more, and be patient until we are unified. Guess what? I hate the red light. Ann really likes it. Remember? I drive with a foot on the gas! No surprise that I like green lights! Ann drives with a foot on the brake, so it's no wonder she likes the red light!

A few years back, I made up my mind that I needed a new business suit. I felt it was way past time to upgrade from the suit I had been wearing. You see, I had inherited a business suit from a man who died unexpectedly—twenty-five years earlier! His son could not wear his father's suits since they were not the right size, so he gave one to me. It fit like a glove and I had been wearing it for twenty-five years. That's two and a half decades! I am giving you a little taste of the argument I made to Ann about why I needed a new suit. In my mind it was no longer a want, but a need. I had been wearing my one and only suit year after year after year. But I suppose I should mention that it was not just any old suit. It was a Giorgio Armani and had been handmade in Italy out of a beautiful dark navy, lightweight wool.

So I went to Ann and made my pitch. It went something like this. "Honey" (I always start with a pet name when I want something), "I would like to buy a new suit. I am tired of my old Armani. I found another suit that fits our budget and looks nice on me. Besides, I am being interviewed on that national TV program next week and I think I better get a new suit before then."

Long pause. Ann seldom blurts out a response. She gives it some thought. Remember, she is the thinker in our home. "I don't think that is a good idea, honey," she said.

"What? You don't think it is a good idea? I have worn that suit for twenty-five years! That's nearly three decades! I can't imagine why you don't think it is a good idea to get a new one now!" I hope this is close to the reality of how I responded. Sometimes I give myself too much grace when recalling a rude reaction of mine. Know what I heard next? Guess.

"Red light."

Those words gently rolled from Ann's lips as my mouth fell open in disbelief. I immediately went into full-blown overreaction and began to talk, talk, talk, talk . . . "Red light! RED LIGHT! Did you say red light?"

"Red light. No arguing—remember?" Ann replied, without even a hint of rubbing it in. She really did not think I needed a new suit.

I was in disbelief. "But why?" I retorted. "Why not a green light? I am going on national TV! This is not a want; this is a need!"

Refusing to enter the debate, Ann simply explained her rationale. "You don't need a new suit. The Armani still fits you perfectly. It hasn't gone out of style. And besides, the world is going casual. You only need to wear it a few times a year. You can get by."

"But, honey, I'll be on national TV. People will be looking at me. I want to look my best."

"Sorry. Red light. You agreed to not argue with me when we set up this process. Remember?"

Checkmate. Argument over. My feelings were hurt. In

one sense, she was right. I didn't wear the suit that often but I didn't think she understood that I was really tired of wearing that same suit for so many years. She also mentioned she thought it was best for a man who teaches others about money to "practice what he preaches" about being a good steward. I wore the Giorgio Armani to the interview.

And then something amazing happened.

During the interview, I was seated across from the host at a small round oak table with a glossy finish. The studio set looked like a fine English library, except for the powerful lights and the fact that we wore makeup to keep the shine off our foreheads and noses. A large camera was positioned directly over the host's shoulder so it could zoom in on my face for a close-up during our conversation. There was another camera providing wide-angle shots and one behind me capable of zooming in on the host. There were several monitors displaying the show graphics and commercial breaks to keep us aware of the flow. A woman standing just out of sight near the cameras gave us the silent countdown with her hand and I saw the red lights blink on, indicating the cameras were rolling. We were live and on the air.

After introductions and some brief chitchat, the host asked me a lot of questions about what the Bible says about money. We focused on stewardship, and I shared how important it is to recognize that financial decisions are outside indicators of our inner spiritual condition. I said, "We write our autobiography with our financial choices. Show me what you spend money on and I can show you the priorities in your life."

His follow-up questions went something like this: "Now hold on a minute, Chuck. Those are very convicting words. Let me get this straight. You believe we can look at the outside signs, the things that are visible, and gain insight about where someone's heart is with money? Is that your point?"

"Yes, sir. That is my point."

"Interesting," the host said as he leaned forward in his chair. Then he stretched out his hand to point at the inside of my suit. "I am looking at your suit. Isn't that a Giorgio Armani suit you are wearing? How can you justify teaching on steward-ship while wearing that fancy suit?"

I had little doubt that at that moment the cameras zoomed in on my face. It felt as if the whole world was watching for my reply. In an instant, my face probably flushed with excitement as I leaned forward in my chair and proudly explained to my host and the audience, "Yes, sir! This suit is in fact a Giorgio Armani! But it is not a NEW suit. Sir, it is twenty-five YEARS old! I inherited it from a DEAD MAN! It was absolutely FREE! And I have worn it faithfully for twenty-five years!" I grabbed both of my lapels and straightened my jacket with pride as my wonderful wife's kind words leaped through my mind. Red light. All I could think of were those words and the red lights on the tops of those TV cameras. Inside I was praising God for those two words and my precious wife. Oh, my precious wife. She had been used to save my reputation, once again! I wondered if she was watching at that very moment, waving to me on national TV, and maybe blowing me a kiss, saying, "Red light."

It was as if the Lord had set me up. He showed me that I had been a fool to argue with Ann over her decision. She was my protector and she had made the right call. How grateful I was for her at that very moment. Oh, how undeserving of such a wonderful friend and counselor! God has used her over and over again in my life and He has used this story in a powerful way. In fact, there is even more to this story.

"IT IS OUR GIFT!"

I was in Brazil the first time I ever taught the Red Light, Yellow Light, Green Light Process to help build and unite marriages. I told the suit story and it brought both laughter and tears to the eyes of the large crowd of married couples gathered at the annual University of the Family Conference. When my talk was over, one of the Christian brothers in attendance approached me and said, "Green light!" I wasn't sure what he meant by that.

He said, "Would Ann vote green light for a new suit from Brazil?"

I still wasn't sure what he meant so I said, "No, we have both agreed it is best to keep the Armani suit and resist the temptation to get a new one. I have learned to listen to her counsel."

"No, no, you do not understand," he said with a laugh. "My wife and I want to buy a new suit for you! It is our gift! Will Ann mind if we buy the suit as our gift to you in appreciation for your ministry to us? Will she say green light to that?"

"Of course," I said, "that will fit our budget perfectly! Green light!"

Less than twenty-four hours after sharing the suit story, I was outfitted with a high-end suit designed and tailored for me in Brazil, complete with a dress shirt, silk tie, and matching leather shoes and belt. It is the most comfortable suit (or clothing of any kind) that I have ever had. I love to wear it as I tell the story of how God has provided for me.

On another trip, I was addressing a small group of business leaders in Asia, speaking with both the husbands and wives covering this material about love and money, which is a very big area of pain in Asia. As I shared the story of the Armani suit and the new one God had provided in Brazil, there were again roars of laughter and tears followed by clapping. The story touched many hearts and I was so grateful that God was using it to build unity and save families. As I was leaving the building, a very striking, well-dressed young couple stopped and asked to speak with me. Of course, I was glad to talk with them.

Through our translator the husband shared, "Our family has been touched by Crown's ministry and we are so grateful for this talk today. We have one question: Does your wife own an Armani dress?"

I could tell the couple was looking at me very seriously, waiting for my reply through the translator. I smiled and said, "No, she does not own an Armani or any other designer dresses. Why do you ask?"

My question was returned with another question, "What size is she?" It became obvious they wanted to get my wife a dress. I quickly told my translator to explain that it was not necessary to get my wife a dress but I appreciated their thoughtfulness. They persisted.

My translator said, "They asked me to tell you that they actually work for Giorgio Armani. That is their business. They loved your story of the suit and want Ann to have an Armani dress. It is best that you give them her size if you want it to fit." I tried saying no a few more times, but ultimately felt I could not turn them down as they were so eager to be generous and bless Ann. She now has not one but two Armani dresses; one is an elegant evening gown and the other a more practical cocktail dress. My new suit and her dresses are continual reminders to me to put Proverbs 12:15 into practice: "The way of a fool is right in his own eyes, but a wise man *listens* to advice" (ESV, emphasis added).

I recommend that you add this simple process to the tools you will use to achieve your financial goals and ultimately your life purpose. It is a wonderful exercise in learning humility and building unity in your marriage. But don't agree to it unless you are both serious and will not back out of your commitment to each other!

Another very helpful process for couples with different strengths when it comes to their finances is what I call "Offense and Defense." In any endeavor, whether sports, business, or combat, it is necessary to have both a strong offense and a strong defense to win the contest. Managing your finances is no different. The offense in this context is the partner responsible for generating the income or "scoring the points," while the defense involves paying the bills and managing the budget. So one of your first priorities as a couple is to establish who is best equipped to fill each role and then to assign the financial tasks and responsibilities accordingly. Now, both of you may be working professionals and both of you may be very good at generating income and managing the budget, but I have found that if one of you will take the primary responsibility for each of these roles, unity can be increased.

It will take both your efforts to achieve your financial goals, so evaluate each other's gifts, personalities, and abilities to determine who should do what. In some cases, one spouse is stronger at both offense and defense. But the need for an effective process does not change. And the one who is assigned to offense and defense will need an encouraging assistant! This should be the role of the spouse in cases when one takes responsibility for both strategies.

"BIBLE STUDY BY CANDLELIGHT"

My friends Dinart and Norma Barradas live in Brazil. I have had the privilege of serving with them on a number of my trips to their country. Having heard them share their testimony about what happened when they were leading one of Crown's small-group Bible studies, I knew their story should be in any book about marriage and money.

Dinart is a trained pastor. He is handsome, outgoing, warm, friendly, and loveable. He exudes joy. He loves people deeply and does not try to hide it. Norma is quiet, reserved, and serious, but sweet too. She enjoys Dinart doing all the talking as they share in front of groups holding hands.

"Norma had been praying for me to take care of the family finances for many years," Dinart began. I could tell he was being careful to honor her part of the story. She blushed as he mentioned her name. "But since I was a busy pastor, she had a small business, managed the family, and also took care of all the bills. We were overspending month after month after month, but I did not realize it. Norma ran her own small business and would work hard to make extra money to cover the expense overruns or she would juggle the bills to keep me from having to get involved each month. When she mentioned a few concerns to me, I dismissed it. I did not hear what she was trying to say."

Norma shared that she was very worried about their finances but could not get Dinart's attention long enough to get him to understand that she seriously needed his help, his support, his guidance on how to take care of this. She was under a great deal of stress and praying constantly for the Lord to show her a solution.

"One day, Norma sensed the Lord had answered her prayers. He impressed on her the need to stop covering up the overspending, to stop working overtime and worrying so much. He promised her that if she would stop interfering that He would get my attention." Dinart paused. Although this event was now a number of years in the past, I could tell it still evoked sensitive emotions. "And God kept His promise! It happened as I arrived home from a church meeting for our Wednesday night fellowship group. When I got there, people were already in our house waiting for me. But I noticed something strange when I walked in the door. All the lights were off in the house. So I told Norma, 'Turn on some lights for everyone.'"

He continued, "Norma was very quick to politely explain to me that tonight was a 'special fellowship group' because she had chosen to have the Bible study 'by candlelight.' I laughed and went ahead with the meeting. But inside, I was dying of embarrassment. I knew. I knew what had just happened. Our electricity had been disconnected for non-payment. It was one of the low points of my life because I knew how embarrassed Norma must have been as well. But . . . she covered for me." Dinart was fighting back his tears. Norma could not hold hers back.

Dinart continued with the rest of the story. "After the meeting, Norma opened up and told me that what I suspected was true. Our power had been cut off right before I arrived home. She had been covering for the family and me for almost two years, but she was exhausted and could not do it any longer. She told me about her prayer and the answer."

They both began to smile as he shared what he had said to her then, "You know, Norma, tonight was the low point of my life as a husband and a father. I have let you down. I am ashamed. But I promise you that I will establish a plan and a process to get us on a budget and out of debt so we never have to go through this again. I promise you."

Dinart proceeded to explain that he had no idea how to manage money. He admitted his weakness and that he had placed his dependency totally on Norma rather than on God since the day they were married. At that moment in his life, feeling totally inadequate, the only thing he knew to do was to "cry out to God for help." He said he prayed that since "God promised to help Norma, that He would help me know what to do too."

He asked God to show him how to manage his responsibilities.

Within a month of that desperate prayer, a friend told him about the Crown Financial Ministries Bible study. He enrolled, got serious about what he was learning, and worked to get unified with Norma. Together, they set up a process for him to take over paying the bills and to work toward getting out of debt. It took them four years. He concluded the story by wrapping his arm around Norma as he said, "That was a special fellowship by candlelight. It changed our lives forever." In Norma's case, she was exhausted playing defense because the one doing the most damage to the family budget was supposed to be on her team! She resigned and her move, led by God, worked brilliantly. It turned out that she was much more productive at generating income in her business when she could focus solely on offense. With Dinart stepping up and taking over the defense, they made great progress as a unified team! Today, they are debt-free, own two homes, one of which is rented for extra income, and are able to freely serve God as a joyful, unified couple. They are achieving their financial plans in a difficult economy and thriving in their relationship.

CAN I GET AN ENVELOPE FOR THAT?

Another simple process that can keep any couple on track, whether you have a lot or a little, is the Cash Envelope System. In our digital world, you may prefer to use online tools that can help you allocate your money and track your spending carefully. I have a few helpful mobile tools that I like that you can find in the Recommended Resources section, but there is one key advantage to the cash envelope system. By dividing your monthly income into categories for specific expenses, you create barriers that will alert you *before* you exceed your credit limit, overdraw your checking account, or write a bad check. If you open the envelope containing money for your monthly hair appointment but it is empty because you used that money to buy groceries, then you know you won't be able to get your hair done this month unless you have spent less for the month in another envelope! I know it is old-school. But it works and works well!

One of the best ways to use this system is to divide your monthly budget into two categories, Fixed and Variable Expenses. Fixed expenses are those payments you make each month that do not change, such as your mortgage or rent payment, tithes, savings, car payments, insurance, taxes, or debt repayments. I suggest that you set those expenses up to automatically be paid each month through electronic withdrawals. The remainder of your budget is made up of variable expenses because they fluctuate from month to month depending on your spending habits and choices. I suggest that you manage all variable expenses by using the envelope system. This means you make an envelope for each variable expense, such as groceries, gasoline, eating out, entertainment, clothing, and childcare. Then you place the budgeted amount of cash inside the appropriate envelope. When the funds are gone from the envelope for that month, stop spending unless you have excess money in another envelope that can be moved to the envelope where you have a need. When you have budgeted an accurate estimate for how much to put in each envelope, your spending and budgeting will be under control.

Experts will tell you that this process will help you learn to live on less than you make. Over time, this will lead you to have a surplus each month as your income increases and your expenses decrease. I strongly recommend it for couples who are trying to establish discipline in their spending habits.

My friends Benedict and Fiona recently invited me to their mountain house to celebrate its completion. By God's kindness, they had been able to build a beautiful home overlooking one of the most scenic natural wonders of Asia. The land on which the house was built had belonged to Ben's father, and Ben spent his childhood summers there in a small wood frame and stone house. But Ben and Fiona had remodeled the ancient simple structure and added to it a modern home featuring six bedrooms spread over three levels as well as two beautiful fireplaces. They now used the home to host family gatherings with all their children and grandchildren under one roof, as well as ministry retreats and planning sessions. It was spectacular.

Soon after I arrived, Ben's wife, Fiona, asked me to join the two of them out on the covered back porch. She is a remarkable hostess, always ready to serve her guests with homemade baked goods, fresh coffee, and gracious hospitality. She brought out a plate of her made-from-scratch cookies fresh from the oven and a cup of coffee. The plate and mug were handcrafted pieces made by a local artisan. It was a fantastic setting and a memorable moment of absolute pleasure.

As we all sat comfortably around the large wicker table, Fiona opened the conversation. "I would like to tell you what made all of this possible, Chuck. I think our story could help lots of young couples who may think money grows on trees."

I replied with a broad grin, "I am not overly concerned with what we talk about, so long as you keep the cookies and coffee coming!"

Fiona glanced at the glorious view from her back porch and explained with genuine humility, "We paid for all this with cash. We don't owe a penny on the mountain house. Although, I prefer to call it God's Mountain House because He owns it all."

She added, "Of course, these breathtaking views were created by Him too!"

I asked, "Were you and Ben rich to be able to afford this home?"

She laughed. "People think because Ben is a doctor we just buy whatever we want. But we don't have any debt and are able to be radically generous with our money. But we were broke when we got married. I mean it. We had nothing!" I could tell she had never forgotten those lean early years of their marriage as she reached down beneath the table to take something out of her purse.

She handed me a white envelope with the title "Beauty shop for Fiona" written on it in large black lettering. "This is our secret, Chuck; these little envelopes with cash inside each one. Want to see them all? I still carry them in my purse. I have for almost fifty years now."

I took the envelope in my hand as Fiona continued. "When we got married, Ben wanted to go to medical school. He told me we could not do it if we spent too much money. I knew it was his calling and so to avoid all the stress of medical school and marriage and a possible pregnancy along the way, we decided to live frugally and use the envelope system Ben's dad taught him. In fact, his grandfather had used this method too. We would just divide up what money we had into these white envelopes and write on them what we could allocate toward our needs like groceries, gas, and rent."

"And *Fiona's Beauty Shop*," I said with a laugh as I held up the envelope she handed me.

"Look, that is not a joke. I told Ben that I would live on this system so long as he promised me one thing—that I could get my hair done twice a month! That was very important to me. Still is to this day!" Fiona pointed to the envelope in my hand. "I haven't stopped using this method since the day we got married. It works! God has blessed our entire lives to avoid the major money problems that hurt so many families."

Ben affirmed her words, patted her on the hand, and added a few of his own thoughts. "Chuck, when we first took the Crown class, we were already good with money. I was taught how to be frugal and we have used these envelopes for generations now in my family. But I never dreamed that if we kept being frugal just how much God would allow us to give to His causes. This house is the only time we have really splurged on ourselves, but we did it for the family too. It will be passed on to our children just like my daddy passed it on to me for our use. We are all just stewards of what God gives us."

SOME FINAL INSIGHTS ON ENCOURAGEMENT

Remember that encouragement is necessary to defeat discouragement. We are all encouraged when we overcome setbacks and challenges. Paul wrote about the process that enables us to move forward when we are in pain in Romans 5:1–5:

> Therefore, since we have been justified through faith, we have peace with God through our Lord Jesus Christ, through whom we have gained access by faith into this grace in which we now stand. And we boast in the hope of the glory of God. Not only so, but we also glory in our sufferings, because we know that suffering produces perseverance; perseverance, character; and character, hope. And hope does not put us to shame, because God's love has been poured out into our hearts through the Holy Spirit, who has been given to us.

Here is a look at the journey through discouragement to hope:

1. We begin with *Peace with God* that comes through faith and grace.
2. Next we experience *Suffering*. (This comes in many forms. Use one of your personal experiences here.)
3. Suffering leads to the opportunity to *Persevere*. This means you don't quit moving forward by faith when you experience heartbreak or a financial setback or a relational problem. Nobody "perseveres" through their Hawaiian vacation! However, a weightlifter must experience pain and persevere through it in order to increase strength. The saying, "No pain, no gain" has some truth to it when it comes to exercise.
4. Perseverance will produce *Character*. That means you develop internal strength to carry you through hardships. A friend describes "character" as a person who is like a tree that has such deep roots in Christ that it can endure a massive storm without being toppled.
5. Character gives us *Hope*. We are ready for the future, encouraged and hopeful when we no longer fear what may come.

To begin working on a financial process that will keep you encouraged and on plan, complete the important practical exercises outlined for you in chapter 9.

We have now covered all seven keys: Peacemaking, Prosperity, Purpose, Philosophy, Personality, Plan, and Process. Now it is time for some inspiration. We've named our next chapter "Marriages That Give Us All Hope." Read on and meet some couples who learned anew how to love, serve, and care for each other. Regardless of where you are now, be sure to read this chapter to prepare you for those unexpected storms that can appear (or reappear) and cause you and your spouse to lose hope. And don't forget, we stand ready to serve you in your journey to align your finances and unite your hearts. You can subscribe to daily devotionals, access free materials, and stay in touch with us at crown.org.

CHAPTER EIGHT

Marriages That Give Us All Hope

*Two are better than one, because they
have a good return for their labor: If either
of them falls down, one can help the other up.*

ECCLESIASTES 4:9–10

CHARLES M. "CHARLIE" Duke Jr. is an American success story. As an accomplished engineer, US Air Force officer, test pilot, and astronaut, Mr. Duke was selected as the Lunar Module Pilot for the Apollo 16 mission. In April 1972, he became the tenth person, and youngest, to walk on the surface of the moon. His resume is filled with accomplishments including multiple awards and degrees and he has been featured in multiple movies, books, and stories. When Charlie returned from the Apollo 16 mission, he was welcomed home by millions as a hero; six years after his successful moon landing, he became a committed Christian.

I had the honor of meeting General Duke briefly after he spoke to a Christian men's group in Dallas, Texas. At that event, he shared his personal testimony and answered the question so many had asked: "What led him from a churchgoer to a fully committed Christian?" I vividly remember Mr. Duke explaining that while he was on the moon he was not thinking about God at all, he was thinking only about doing his job. In fact, it was not the trip to the moon that led him to surrender his life fully to Christ but rather, it was the realization after he got back that, apart from God's help, he "couldn't get along with his wife."

The room filled with laughter. His confession caused almost every one of us to feel an odd sense of relief. The seeming paradox of a man so highly accomplished, yet humbly acknowledging that his greatest struggle was in his marriage, helped give comfort to others who had fallen flat on their faces in their marriages. Anyone, husband or wife, who has been through such a trial knows all too well that one of the highest forms of pain is to be hurt by or cause harm to those we actually love.

The laughter quickly subsided and the mood became serious when Charlie explained how this challenge in his marriage had brought him to his knees. He shared poignantly how he had achieved all of his ambitious life goals while mostly relying upon himself. When he returned from his successful space mission, he found his wife, Dotty, depressed and contemplating suicide. The demands of his career and the way he had put himself first had taken a toll on his wife as she quietly dealt with the challenges of raising their two young boys on her own. Charlie was a hero to the world, but not to Dotty. She felt hurt, lonely, and trapped. After trying many options in looking for relief from her pain, she turned to God. Only when she placed her full faith in and derived her acceptance from Jesus Christ was she able to conquer the overwhelming despair and hopelessness. She gained a new identity. She was still the wife of one of America's great heroes, but more importantly, she was a child of God Almighty.

Charlie continued his testimony, explaining that he realized he needed God to help him change, to be able to understand and be united with his wife. Dotty's testimony helped him recognize that he had simply been a churchgoer and that he needed to fully surrender everything to Jesus Christ. Since that moment, by the power of God, Charlie and Dotty have kept their vows, become united, and overcome the storms threatening their marriage.[1]

As Charles and Dotty Duke discovered, navigating the challenges of keeping your marriage vows can be a great struggle. And it is a struggle that may drive us to the end of our own abilities and capacity, no matter how great they may be. If you have read the rest of this book yet remain deeply concerned over the collision of many storms in your marriage, I invite you to turn to Jesus Christ. Ask Him to come into your life and take over, to transform you into a new creation. Turn from your sins, mistakes, and failures and seek with all your heart to be conformed into His image. Commit to pray and read the Bible. Commit your marriage to His loving care. If you have never done so before, join me now in praying this prayer:

> Lord Jesus, I need You. I confess my sins to You and turn from my unbelief. I ask You to come into my life and make me into a new creation. Thank You for forgiving me for my sins, mistakes, and failures. Conform me into Your image. Give me the strength to be a loving and kind spouse and a faithful steward of our finances. I place my life in Your hands and submit my will to the control of the Holy Spirit. In Jesus' name, amen.

The truth is you will not be able to unite in your marriage or be aligned in your finances unless you are drawn closer to Jesus. He will give you the strength to keep your vows when you are suffering. He will unite you in love, bring solutions to your financial challenges, and restore joy to your marriage. Jesus will make your marriage richer, help you align your finances, and make two very different people into one. Marriages flourish when both husband and wife know the Way, the Truth, and the Life.

In my years of working with Crown, I have seen God intervene in miraculous ways to turn marriages around in an instant. Here are a couple more stories of "marriage miracles"—I hope they inspire and encourage you.

I have shared some of those powerful stories with you already. Distressed marriages take time and perseverance to heal, but we have sought to encourage you by sharing situations when lies were exposed, truth embraced, and couples liberated from the storms that had battered their relationship. In sharing a few more, I intend to give you hope, regardless of your current circumstances or the pain you might be experiencing right now.

A Public Plea for Help

"I need your help." Jean, the woman sitting next to me at the head table of a large formal evening banquet uttered those words so softly I had to ask her to repeat what she said. I smiled at her while glancing over her shoulder to see if her husband, seated next to her, was paying attention to our conversation. He was not.

"What did you say?" I asked quietly, unsure if I had heard her correctly.

"I need your help . . . now."

Those words took me completely by surprise, but not as much as what was to follow. Although I now understood what she had said, I was unsure how to respond. We were at a large public event in Asia, dinner was being served, and I was supposed to give a speech in ten minutes! I could not process my response. Her plea had come out of nowhere.

I managed to say, "Uh, uh . . . okay, what do you need help with?" Her husband, George, was talking with the person next to him and I tried to get his attention and engage him in the conversation. But he did not stop talking and was sitting with his back turned to his wife and me.

Suddenly, she had my undivided attention as she burst into tears and abruptly declared, "I need your help with our marriage!" She took the linen napkin that had once been in her lap and used it to cover her face as the dam of emotion burst.

As if he had been struck by lightning, George turned around, his eyes darting between Jean, now sobbing loudly, and me, looking more stunned than ever, and the people around us, who were obviously wondering what had just happened. I will never forget the look on George's face as his smile melted into a look of panic and the color drained from his face.

For a wife to publicly expose a marriage problem was a huge "loss of face" and totally unacceptable to her husband. I would not have liked it myself. What had just happened would have been embarrassing in any culture. The evening was now completely in jeopardy. How were we going to manage this crisis and continue the scheduled events?

My adrenalin seemed to kick into high gear. I had one speech left to give on this trip, which was now due to start in just nine minutes. George was supposed to speak after me, then we would wrap up the event, I would get some sleep and catch the first plane home in the morning. That plan appeared to be out the window. Would I be giving George's speech too? Should we cancel the meeting now? I prayed hard and asked the Lord to intervene.

Before either George or I could say a word, Jean continued.

> HOW WERE WE GOING TO MANAGE THIS CRISIS AND CONTINUE THE SCHEDULED EVENTS? I PRAYED HARD AND ASKED THE LORD TO INTERVENE.

"Our marriage is in ruins. I cannot take it anymore. I cannot go another day in this pain. You must help us or we will not survive as man and wife."

"I understand, Jean. I understand," I assured her.

George had moved in closer and placed his arm around Jean's shoulder. I patted her shoulder as well. She was regaining her composure when I came up with an idea. "It appears we need to talk together at length. We need more time than we have right now. How about we meet early for breakfast and talk before I fly back home tomorrow? How do you feel about that?"

She dabbed her eyes with the corner of her napkin, sniffed a time or two, and sat up straight in her chair. "Yes, that would be good. I know this is not the right time to talk. I am sorry to have done this. Please forgive me."

Jean was embarrassed, but obviously a very heartbroken woman. I was encouraged that the intensity of the moment had died down, but the pain was still written on both of their faces. I had no idea how I was going to pull my thoughts together to deliver my talk (now starting in six minutes) but I especially had no idea how George was going to speak next. Looking back, it was only God's grace that enabled us to deliver our talks successfully.

We had arranged to meet in my hotel at half past six the next morning, where a buffet-style breakfast was served. I had to leave for the airport at nine o'clock. I found a quiet table in a far corner. Jean and George walked into the restaurant together, which was a good sign, although I could tell by their faces that there had been no improvement in their relation-ship during the night. After they sat down, I led the three of us in prayer. As soon as I finished, Jean said she wanted to say something.

"I want to first apologize to my husband for what I did last night. It was wrong. He has such high regard for you, Mr. Chuck, that it was a terrible embarrassment for me to say what I said and to interrupt the event like I did." She turned to George. "Will you please forgive me for bringing a loss of face to you last night?"

George and Jean are both deeply committed Christians. I was very hopeful that he would respond well to her sincere apology. And he did. "Yes. I forgive you." He did not demand an explanation or make condemning comments, which he must have felt were due him. He patted her on the arm.

Our meeting went well. I discovered that Jean's main struggle was a deep sense of loneliness and isolation. George was busy. He was not great at one-on-one conversation or being sensitive to her needs. Jean did not feel like she was a part of his life. She felt she had all the responsibility for their home and children but no relationship with her husband. He traveled extensively and other women from the company were often on the trips. She felt very insecure, and he did not slow down long enough to understand what she was feeling.

We worked through the principles of making peace and bringing harmony to their home. They committed to follow the principles I have shared with you in this book. I was able to put Jean in contact with Ann so she would receive more sup-port. That conversation was five years ago. George and Jean's relationship began to heal that morning, and steadily improved to where they are now: leading others to understand God's way of marriage.

I also want to highlight a pivotal moment in the restoration of this couple and their family. Can you identify it? Hint: it has nothing to do with me. When Jean humbled herself and apologized to George, in my presence, and asked for his forgiveness, it changed the entire dynamic of the meeting. Don't miss this. When George accepted her apology, I knew they would make great progress. As I discussed in chapter 1, humility met a response of humility. Both of their hearts were open to forgive and to listen to each other. Remember Proverbs 15, "A gentle answer turns away wrath, but grievous words stir up anger" (v. 1 KJV). Jean and George were both hurting, but Jean chose the path of humility. Her actions remind me of the promise in 1 Peter: "Clothe yourselves, all of you, with humility toward one another, for 'God opposes the proud but gives grace to the humble.' Humble yourselves, therefore, under the mighty hand of God so that at the proper time he may exalt you, casting all your anxieties on him, because he cares for you" (5:5–7 ESV).

Jean humbled herself, entrusting the outcome to God, and He gave her grace. He gave George grace. And He gave grace to a family of four that is now thriving.

Saving the Home, Not Just the House

"Mr. Bentley, I need your advice on how to avoid a foreclosure on my home."

The caller on the phone was a total stranger to me; her opening comment was brief and matter-of-fact. Her soft-spoken, polite manner indicated that I was speaking with a young lady who sounded sincere and unusually calm given her plight. This call was taking place on my nationwide radio program, *My Money-Life*, and I knew there were thousands of listeners waiting for my response (and perhaps in the same crisis themselves). I felt the pressure to give her a solid answer. While waiting for my reply, this young woman, whom I'll call Francine, added, "I'm behind on my mortgage payments. What should I do?"

The question seemed to hang in the air as seconds of dead silence ticked by. It was 2010 and millions of Americans were facing a financial crisis as home values plunged due to the Great Recession. The federal government had recently introduced a number of programs to help homeowners who were "under water" or "upside down" on their mortgage, which are terms used to describe the condition of owing more on a home loan than the house is worth. In some of the hardest-hit states, as many as 50 percent of the home loans made in the previous eight years fell into this "under water" category.

I was about two years into broadcasting a nationwide call-in program on Christian radio in the United States, a program that had been founded twenty years earlier by the late Larry Burkett, who was known for his expert and biblical financial advice. I always tried to keep an array of helpful resources as well as relevant Scripture at my fingertips so I would be ready to address the needs of each caller. My job was to be discerning and helpful to every person on the other end of the line but not to get bogged down with too many details, because that makes for bad radio and usually doesn't transfer well in a time-condensed format.

So although I was well equipped to give practical advice to this caller, I felt the Holy Spirit was whispering in my ear not to give a "man's economy" reply but instead to offer help based upon the principles of "God's economy." I decided to answer her question with a question of my own. "Hi, Francine, thanks for calling today. I am happy to try to help you avoid foreclosure but first, tell me a little bit about your situation. Can I get a few more details before I offer my counsel?" I remained upbeat in order to convey a sense of hope and encouragement in my voice.

Francine did not hesitate. "Sure! We are three months behind on our mortgage. Our lender sent us a letter that said if we don't make a payment soon, they will start the process to legally remove us from the house. I need to know what to do next."

I picked up on the word *we* in her statement and I responded, "So are you married, Francine?"

"Yes, I'm married, but my husband has left me. He wants a divorce. I have a four-year-old at home and I am pregnant with twins," Francine said without any tone of bitterness or self-pity. "It's urgent that I know what to do next since I am totally on my own to deal with this."

My heart sank. I suddenly realized that Francine had a much bigger problem than a possible foreclosure. Her entire life was about to come apart at the seams. All I could think of was the plight of her children and the home that would not be there for all three of them. Not the house, but the home. I was overcome with compassion for Francine, her child, and the twins on their way. I knew this was not the time to turn her over to a federal agency to try to save the house. God was nudging me out of my comfort zone to try to save the marriage.

"Francine." I spoke with a very gentle voice hoping to avoid overstepping my bounds. "If you don't mind, I would like to speak to you privately about your situation. I think I can help you, but we don't have enough time during today's program to talk about it on the air. Is that okay with you?"

"Sure! Do you want me to just hang on the line?" she said.

"That would be great. Hang on."

I wrapped up the program, signed off the air, and picked up Francine's call once more. What happened next can only be described as God's divine intervention.

God gave me the courage to speak to Francine in a simple

yet direct way, to give her a plan to save her marriage. My first request was to arrange for a conference call with Francine *and* her husband, whom I'll call Joe. I wanted to speak to them both about the importance of saving their marriage and give them a process for how they could unify and save their house. Francine said, "That will never happen. Joe has left. He doesn't want to talk to me anymore. He won't talk to a counselor, a pastor, and especially not to me. He said the house is my problem. He won't talk to anybody about this. Not even you."

As it turned out, Joe, a career military man, did agree to talk. In our call the next day, he told me he had just recently returned from a long deployment. Francine had taken over the management of the finances while he was away. When he returned, their bills and credit were in disarray. He said, "She is terrible with money! I asked her if I could take over and she told me, 'No way, I have had to do this by myself for so long, I will take care of it.'" At that point, Joe told Francine she had created the mess and that he was leaving.

Francine confirmed the accuracy of Joe's account. After sharing this story, they both went silent, waiting on me to speak. I took a deep breath and spent the next hour sharing as much as possible from the principles in this book. When I finished, neither of them said a word. I felt like I had spoken to a concrete wall, wasting a full hour of our time. I promised to send them each a few books and if they agreed to read them, I would meet with them again and talk about the foreclosure issue.

I sent them the books, several of which are listed in the Recommended Resources at the end of this book. A week went by and the call we had scheduled was on my calendar. I dialed the conference number not sure if either Francine or Joe would dial in. But Joe was the first on the call.

"Hello, Mr. Bentley. It's me, Joe."

The upbeat tone of his voice surprised me. I replied, "Great. Thanks for calling in today. Did you read the books I sent you?"

"Yes, sir. I read them and they helped a lot."

This was encouraging. I said, "That's great. I am hoping Francine read the books as well and will call in today."

"Uh, Mr. Bentley," he said, "Francine is on the line with me. I have moved back home."

Hope and excitement flooded my heart. *Could it be true?* I thought to myself as Joe politely continued. "Neither of us want a divorce and we realized that we really love each other. Francine and I want to make this work."

I was silent, but praising God to myself as he shared more of the story.

"She apologized . . . and we are committed to make this work." He paused. "Uh, can we talk about this foreclosure problem . . . like, today?"

Tears welled up in my eyes. I was almost speechless. Francine broke the silence, "Mr. Bentley, I can't thank you enough. We are committed to working through this. We think we can do this . . . together."

Joe and Francine both sounded different, the joy in both their voices like a spring breeze that had swept their hearts clean of the anger, fear, and bitterness I had sensed before. Weeks later I received another call notifying me that the twins had been born, they were current on their mortgage, and Joe and Francine were getting along great and making progress with all their financial challenges.

Francine's story ends well. She was reconciled with her husband, had avoided foreclosure, and was thriving after the birth of the twins. The root issue in their marriage was small but it had created a toxic mixture of division, conflict, and rejection. But this encounter gave me hope that restoration is possible when both spouses are willing to unite and tackle their problems.

I believe the Holy Spirit was teaching me that the home (the marriage and family) was more important than the house. By saving the marriage, we were able to save everything else.

In the years since that call, I have learned the profound truth that "it is not good that the man should be alone," and that when God created woman as a helper for man, it was a massive symbol of His gift and blessing to the world (Gen. 2:18–25). He gave the man a woman to minister to his needs and give him joy. He gave the woman a man that will minister to her needs and give her joy. The greatest blessing and financial advantage for a man or woman is a happy marriage. It is getting to the "happy" part that will require work on both your parts.

KEEP HOPING, KEEP WORKING

If your relationship is currently strained or badly damaged, even if you are the only spouse willing to work on your marriage now, I highly recommend that you begin to apply the seven keys we have shared in the previous chapters and begin to pray for a breakthrough in your marriage. The Bible says that when we suffer, we learn to persevere. When we persevere, our character increases (Rom. 5:3–4). This means that when we don't quit when we feel like quitting, our inner strength becomes stronger than before. When our character is strong, we have hope. Hope will not put us to shame because of the love God has showered upon us (Rom. 5:5). May God bring you this depth of hope right now, regardless of your circumstances. Trust Him that your relationship and financial issues can be resolved and even redeemed. Remember, to experience this hope, you will need to persevere and cast your cares upon the Lord when you feel like giving up.

With all of our hearts, Ann and I plead with you not to lose hope and to remember the Lord's promise that two are in fact better than one. Contrary to popular belief, marriage is ordained by God for your good. Now, get about the hard work of saving and strengthening your marriage.

In the final chapter, Ann and I have prepared a series of practical applications for you and your spouse to work through together as well as a special vow so you can commit to putting the seven keys into practice. May God align your finances, unite your hearts in love, and bless you as the two of you become one.

CHAPTER NINE

Going Deeper

If you know these things, blessed are you if you do them.

JOHN 13:17 ESV

There is no more lovely, friendly, and charming relationship, communion or company than a good marriage.

MARTIN LUTHER

THE PRINCIPLES and insights you have read about are totally useless until they are put into practice. Below are discussion questions and other exercises for each of the seven keys to help you think more deeply about the content of the book. Following completion of the practical applications, turn to Our Money and Marriage Vow on page 153 so that you and your spouse can make a record of your mutual commitment to unity and alignment. I have also included a chart at the end of this chapter so you can track your progress through the homework.

KEY #1
COMMIT TO BECOMING A PEACEMAKER

Mark 10:9 is a call to fight for peace: "What therefore God has joined together, let not man separate" (ESV). The forces of hell are waging a war to destroy your peace and rob you of the unity, joy, and satisfaction God wants for your marriage. Work through the content below to grow by becoming a peacemaker.

Memorize Matthew 5:9 and discuss the following questions:

How does this verse relate to your responsibility in your marriage? With your children? In your business?

Read 1 Corinthians 13 together and discuss the following questions:

1. In what ways have you seen this description of love exhibited in God's love for you?
2. How can resting in God's unconditional love for you free you to share this kind of love with others?
3. What does love have to do with bringing peace to your marriage?
4. What aspects of this description of love do you need to put into practice?
5. Ask your spouse how you can better exhibit 1 Corinthians love to them.
6. Have you ever used an excuse to justify your anger or failed to take responsibility for bad behavior? If so, take the opportunity to repent now.

Memorize the poem "First" and post it somewhere in your home where both you and your spouse will see it regularly.

> *The first to apologize is the bravest.*
> *The first to forgive is the strongest.*
> *The first to forget is the happiest.*

KEY #2
GRASP THE BIBLICAL DEFINITION OF PROSPERITY

Read Jeremiah 29:5–11 and fill in the blanks with the biblical *prosperity* principles.

- Build _____ and settle down.
- _____ _____ and eat what they produce.
- _____ and have _____ and
  _____.
- Find wives for your sons and give your daughters in
  marriage so they too may have _____ and
  _____.
- _____ in number. Do not
  _____.
- Seek the _____ and _____ of the city.
- _____ to the Lord for it, because if it
  prospers, you too will prosper.
- Do not let the prophets and diviners among you _____
  _____ you.

Discuss the following questions with your spouse:

1. How are we doing in following God's definition of
   prosperity?
2. How does the Law of Inverse Prosperity apply to you
   and your spouse?
3. What city will you begin to pray for its peace and
   prosperity?
4. What information or teaching will you reject that does
   not agree with God's Word?
5. How has God instructed you to pray for your family?
   Has God put adoption on your heart?

KEY #3
KNOW AND FULFILL YOUR LIFE PURPOSE

If you and your spouse had the opportunity to write your obituary in three bullet points right now, how do you think you would be remembered?

-
-
-

Read 2 Chronicles 16:9. What does it say about those who have fully surrendered to God?

Can you say with Nick Vujicic that you are a "willing heart" when it comes to allowing God to control your life? Why or why not?

How would you hope to repurpose your life?

Use the three recommended tools: Know Thyself, the Sound-Mind Principle, and the Trust and Obey Method to determine God's specific calling on your life.

Spend some time sharing with each other about your gifts and talents, then discuss these questions to help you think through what you are uniquely called by God to accomplish. Commit these questions to prayer and wise counsel. Don't allow business or fear or finances to create a stumbling block. He will show you His desire for your life. I also recommend that you both participate in a Career Direct Assessment to help you identify your personality, skills, interests, and values. This will help you determine your life purpose.

What do you do that gives you the most joy?

What do others most often affirm that you do very well?

What scriptures most speak to your heart?

How could the world be most improved by your service?

As a couple, we want you to prepare a written purpose statement. First, pray together and ask the Lord to reveal His purpose for you as a couple. Do not rush this. Then write out your purpose statement, striving to be as specific and concise as possible.

God's purpose for our lives is to bring Him glory by:

_____

_____

The verse that best defines our life purpose is:

_____.

KEY # 4
LIVE BY GOD'S PHILOSOPHY OF MONEY

Which of the financial issues identified in the *USA Today* survey do you struggle with most?

How have you seen two very different philosophies of money at work in your marriage?

Read Romans 12:1–2. Have your financial beliefs been more conformed to the world or to God's Word? According to this passage, how does transformation take place?

Memorize 1 Chronicles 29:11–12 together.

Complete the free MoneyLife Indicator Assessment: http://info.crown.org/indicator. Once completed, examine your personal beliefs and consider the areas that are not in alignment with God's Word. Compare your report with your spouse's or that of your future spouse to see where you have significant differences. I also highly recommend that you and your spouse participate in a MoneyLife Personal Financial Bible Study. Learn more at https://engage.crown.org/moneylife-self-paced/.

What verse or verses most accurately summarizes your personal financial philosophy? Record them here.

_____

_____

KEY # 5
UNDERSTAND AND RESPECT
YOUR SPOUSE'S PERSONALITY

Read Ephesians 2:10 and discuss the following questions.

How does this verse apply to you?

How does this verse apply to your spouse?

How does this verse apply to you as a couple?

Complete a personality assessment for couples. Review your results with each other and consider discussing them with a trusted advisor such as a pastor or counselor to better understand each other.

Discuss some of the specific ways you and your spouse differ. Talk about the ways each of you fills in the areas where one of you is lacking. How can each of you be more kind, sensitive, and understanding of your differences?

Plan for a date night or a quiet evening when just the two of you can sit and discuss your personalities and how important you are to one another. Pray together, giving thanks for the unique masterpiece that God has created in the one you love.

KEY #6
CREATE A UNIFIED FINANCIAL PLAN

Which couple in this chapter do you most relate to? Why?

Have you ever been overwhelmed by debt or financial pressures?

Which of you is more likely to want to make a plan?

Read Proverbs 16:3 and Proverbs 21:5. What do these verses speak to your hearts? How can you put these principles into action?

Set aside some time during the week or on weekends to get away and make your financial plan. Keep in mind the unified purpose statement you developed. Now write your short- and long-term financial goals making sure to include a measurable outcome, a target completion date, and a method to accomplish that goal. (Example: We will begin giving 10 percent of our annual income to support God's kingdom beginning next month by reducing our entertainment spending and paying off debt.)

Begin giving _____ (% of income) by _____ (date). This will be accomplished by _____ (method).

Save $1,000 in an emergency savings account by _____ (date). This will be accomplished by _____ (method).

Add $_____ (equal to 3–6 months' worth of living expenses) to emergency savings account by _____ (date). This will be accomplished by _____ (method).

Reduce all consumer debt by _____ (date). This will be accomplished by_____ (method).

Increase our savings another $_____ by _____ (date). This will be accomplished by _____ (method).

Increase our investments to $_____ by _____ (date). This will be accomplished by_____ (method).

We will complete our estate plans and documents by _____ (date).

What rewards or celebrations will you use to stay motivated and focused on this journey?

If you knew you would only be able to achieve one goal in the next year, which one is the most important for you? Which one is the least important?

KEY #7
ESTABLISH A PROCESS THAT ENSURES SUCCESS

Read 1 Corinthians 14:40. How can this verse be applied to the way you manage your finances?

> What example of an orderly process can you find in the Bible and how might you use that process to achieve your financial goals and fulfill your life purpose?

> Which of the processes covered in this chapter did you find most helpful? Discuss which of them you might implement in your own marriage.

> Develop a monthly budget, making sure to divide your expenses into fixed and variable. Consider using the cash envelope system or another process to manage your expenses and bring your spending under control. If you use a digital budgeting program or software, work toward ensuring that both of you are using it effectively.

> Go away for a short weekend and continue establishing financial goals, then spend time updating your financial records, will, and estate documents. Consider the "Blueprint for Your Family Finances" from Crown as the basis for your workbook to store all of your important records.

KEY	ACTION	RECOMMENDED RESOURCE	HOMEWORK COMPLETION	VOW COMPLETION
Peacemaker	Be first to apologize	*The 5 Love Languages*; *Sacred Marriage*; *Love and Respect*		
Prosperity	Adopt God's definition	*The Root of Riches*; The MoneyLife Personal Finance Study		
Purpose	Unite around common vision	Career Direct		
Philosophy	Align your beliefs with Scripture	MoneyLife Indicator		
Personality	Become a 360° marriage	Personality ID for Couples		
Plan	Follow the Money Map; build a budget	Crown.org: budget; Money Map; Blueprint for Family Finances; The MoneyLife Personal Finance Study; MoneyLife Mentor		
Process	Implement a process to follow	Envelope system; Debt snowball calculator; Red Light, Yellow Light, Green Light		

Our Money and Marriage Vow

Today I, _____ and I, _____ (fill in your first names) acknowledge our mutual desire to be *peacemakers*, not troublemakers. Because we want to experience the true shalom God has promised, we commit to humble ourselves and to strive to be the first to apologize, the first to forgive, and the first to forget. We will practice the peacemaking principles covered in chapter 1, so that we can overcome the struggle of constant conflict.

We pledge to unify as husband and wife to follow God's *prosperity* plan. From this day forward, our efforts to build our family's prosperity will be according to God's ways. We agree to establish a place to live so that we can settle down and build our family. We agree to work and build our income so that we are not reliant on others for our food and provision. We agree, while recognizing God's sovereignty over the womb, that children are a blessing from the Lord and the source of true riches. If we are blessed with children, we agree to raise them in a godly home and prepare our sons and daughters to marry. We agree to pray regularly for and seek the peace of the city where God has established our family. We acknowledge that our own prosperity will come from our willingness to help others prosper.

We commit to be unified in seeking God's *purpose* for us as individuals and as a couple, living out that God-ordained purpose to glorify Him and enjoy Him forever.

We commit to looking to God's Word and living by His *philosophy* of money. We affirm that we have sought the Scripture and made His financial philosophy our own.

We acknowledge that while our *personalities* are different, each of us is fearfully and wonderfully made by God. We agree that, although we each respond to our environment and circumstances differently, we have an advantage together because we recognize that our differences are a benefit to each other rather than a hindrance. Together, we affirm to each other that we have been made into a complete and whole unit, joined together by God for our good and His glory. We hereby pledge before God our Creator that we accept each other as He made us. We will strive to protect our unity as we show kindness, patience, grace, and acceptance toward each other.

We commit our unified financial *plan* to the Lord, trusting Him to bring about His will according to Proverbs 16:3. We commit to be diligent and work hard, asking the Lord to give us focus, self-control, discipline, and faithfulness as we work to accomplish our short- and long-term financial goals and overcome confusion.

We mutually agree that we need to have the discipline to follow a *process* to align our finances and achieve our financial and life goals. We commit to be honest, transparent, and open in our communications with each other and to avoid arguments, manipulation, or any deception. We come together, before the Lord, to unify as one and work together to follow through with the plans He has given us by using the tools and methods that best suit our strengths. We will give our best efforts to be disciplined and focused as we seek the Lord to give us grace, patience, perseverance, and courage.

By God's grace and His Holy Spirit, we ask for healing, humility, and unending love according to 1 Corinthians 13. We agree to seek God and trust His Word as our authority on all matters regarding our personal relationship with Him, our marriage, our finances, and our family.

Signed _____

Dated _____

Recommended Resources

The 5 Love Languages, by Dr. Gary Chapman

The 5 Love Languages Assessment:
http://www.5lovelanguages.com/profile/

When Sorry Isn't Enough, by Dr. Gary Chapman
and Dr. Jennifer Thomas

Sacred Marriage, by Gary Thomas

Love and Respect, by Dr. Emerson Eggerichs

The MoneyLife Personal Finance Study by Crown
Financial Ministries. Online at http://info.crown.org
/onlinestudy

MoneyLife Indicator Assessment—https://mli.
crown.org

Blueprint for Your Family Finances—Crown.org

The Root of Riches, by Chuck Bentley

*The Worst Financial Mistakes in the Bible and How You
Can Avoid Them,* by Chuck Bentley

God Is Faithful, by Larry Burkett and Chuck Bentley

Love Your Work, by Robert Dickie III

The Money Map Companion Guide—Crown Financial
Ministries

Online/Digital Tools

All Crown resources: https://www.crown.org/resources/

MoneyLife Indicator: https://engage.crown.org/mli/

Debt Snowball Calculator—Simple and easy to use, this applies the "rollover method" to your debts, helping you pay them off faster and with less interest. https://www.crown.org/resources/debt-snowball-calculator/

Money Map: https://crownfinancial.leadpages.co/money-map-general-download-crown-org/

God is Faithful Daily Devotional: https://www.crown.org/resources/god-is-faithful-daily-devotional/

Personal Finance Calculators—Crown has many financial calculators that can help you reach your goals and make wise decisions with your money. https://www.crown.org/resources/crown-calculators/

MoneyLife Personal Finance Study online: https://www.crown.org/personal-finance/

Career Direct: https://www.crown.org/career/

Budgeting/Tracking Tool: can help you track spending and walks you through the steps to set up a budget that you can live with.—https://planner.crown.org/Default.aspx—This

Crown Radio: https://www.crown.org/radio/

A Case for Marriage and Families

OUR GREAT hope in writing this book is not only to help individual couples but to reverse some of the devastating trends in delayed or broken marriages, declining birthrates, and single-family households. Many of the current trends are occurring because of lies that people believe. We want to expose those lies and equip you with biblical and statistical truth.

One dominant false philosophy of the day proposes that there are too many people on planet Earth and too few resources to go around. This worldview advocates that birth rates need to *decrease* so that prosperity may *increase*. But this is not only a plan for more loneliness, isolation, and selfishness; it will result in an economic disaster. The "children are bad for your prosperity" philosophy is a self-serving and ultimately destructive plan, evidenced by the practice of abortion, delayed marriages, abstaining from marriage, and a preference toward fewer and fewer children in the developed world. This is exactly opposite of God's plan and a blatant lie against God and His Word. Christians are to be "fruitful and multiply" (Gen. 9:7). Marriage and children are good for us, not bad![1]

This callous disregard for our most precious of all assets, children, is seen in the falling birthrates in China, Japan, the United States, Germany, Italy, and nearly all other developed countries.[2] For instance, in Denmark, 50 percent of households consist of just one person. Half of those considered a "family unit" are either singles, childless divorcees, or widows who live alone.[3] In the United States, three-quarters of people surveyed by Gallup said the main reason couples weren't having more children was a lack of money or fear of the economy.[4] The irony is that *not having children* will hurt the economy far more than having children! Economists are worried not just because growth is stalling in working-age populations but because their numbers as a share of the total population in many countries are also falling. Economists like to see this share of total population rise, because it means more people are earning money, expanding the tax base, and paying for schools for the young and pensions and health care for the old.

Before the Great Recession in 2008, the number of these potential workers as a proportion of total population was falling in three of the world's six largest developed economies—Japan, Germany, and Italy. Now the proportion is also dropping in the United States, France, and the United Kingdom, according to data from the United Nations. In 2012, there were twenty-two people age sixty-five and older for every one hundred working-age adults in the United States. By 2030, that ratio is expected to climb to thirty-five older people per one hundred workers.[5]

Economists say it is rare for the number of working-age people as a share of the total population to fall in so many major countries at the same time. This phenomenon is usually because of widespread war or famine, although such proportions also fell in the 1950s as baby boomers were born and populations surged. The six countries with declining proportions of working-age people now, plus China, accounted for 60 percent of global economic output in 2012.[6]

Some very wealthy, very bright people continually evangelize the story line that having fewer children is better for the planet and ultimately provides a path out of poverty. In spite of the obvious devastation this worldview will reap, the unfounded fear of overpopulation has taken root and is widely believed to be true. This godless philosophy should be reclassified as fiction, not fact. Instead of viewing people as mere *consumers*, we must remember that God created humankind to be *producers* as well. Men and women bring new ideas, solve problems, and contribute multiple resources for the benefit of mankind. God has faithfully provided an abundance of resources for the planet beginning with Adam and Eve.

MARRIAGE AND CHILDREN IMPROVE FINANCIAL AND OVERALL WELL-BEING

A careful examination of the benefits of marriage universally proves that, in contrast to all other living arrangements, it is the superior choice. Here are just a few of the facts, which may startle you:

Marriage makes you happier[7]

A number of studies consistently cite marriage as a contributor to overall life satisfaction, while others have sought to refute this claim. What all will agree on is that for those couples who stay married, they consistently report their happiness as greater than before they were married.

Significantly, getting married is part of what has been referred to as the "success sequence": get a high school degree (at least); get a job; get married; start a family. Doing all these things, in this order, markedly improves life prospects for both individuals and families.[8]

Savings soar

"A new survey on retirement spending by T. Rowe Price revealed that many recent retirees are living comfortably and faring well financially, mainly because they have IRAs or 401(k)s. The finding, however, applies for married couples only, as the study found that retirees who are not married or living with a significant other are not doing as well. . . . Almost half (48%) of all single individuals are unsatisfied with their retirement. According to a 2012 study by the National Bureau of Economic Research, the retired, married household had almost **10 times** as much in savings as the typical single-person household"[9] (emphasis added).

Marriage increases your net worth

"What impact do marriage and divorce have on wealth? US data from the National Longitudinal Survey of Youth (NLSY79), which tracks individuals in their 20s, 30s and early 40s, show that over time single respondents slowly increase their net worth. Married respondents experience per-person **net worth increases of 77 percent** over single respondents. Additionally, their **wealth increases on average 16 percent for each year of marriage**. Divorced respondents' wealth starts falling four years before divorce and they experience an average wealth drop of 77 percent. While in percentage terms divorce hurts women more than men, the absolute difference is relatively small in the US"[10] (emphasis added).

Married men earn more than their single counterparts

"Married men make a lot more money than single men. In the NLSY, married men make 44 percent extra, even after controlling for education, experience, IQ, race, and number of children."[11]

Families save more money

The mean net worth of married couple households ($187,102) was substantially higher than that of cohabitant households ($77,093), male-headed households ($92,045), and female-headed households ($48,726), which was the lowest of all family structures.[12]

Married couples report greater sexual satisfaction

Given the amount of critical comments made about the quality or frequency of sex in marriage and other committed relationships, the data support the idea of contented partners. A large majority (88%) of married individuals reported feeling extremely or very satisfied with their physical relationship and having feelings of love after engaging in sexual behaviors. Married respondents, especially those who were monogamous, reported the highest levels of sexual satisfaction, whereas cohabiting and dating couples reported slightly lower levels of satisfaction.[13]

Marriage increases the likelihood of affluence[14]

On average, married-couple families accumulate significantly more assets than female-headed households. The level of assets in married-couple households (both financial and non-financial) was nearly four times as great as the level of assets for female-headed households.[15]

Marriage is associated with a lower mortality risk

Over the course of eight years, the odds of mortality were 58 percent higher for never-married individuals, 27 percent for divorced/separated individuals, and 39 percent for widowed individuals, compared to married individuals.[16]

Married women experience less poverty[17]

On average, married couples are less likely than cohabiting couples to be in poverty. The income-to-needs ratios, which measure family economic resources (family income divided by poverty threshold), were higher for married men and women than for cohabiting couples. The likelihood that married couples were in poverty was 9 to 11 percent lower compared to cohabiting couples.

Men with kids earn more income than single counterparts[18]

According to a new study, men with kids earned a median salary of $49,000, while men without kids earned a median salary of only $29,000. Men with kids also earned twice as much as women with children. Dads earn 41 percent more than childless men.

COMMIT TO A COMMITTED MARRIAGE

As you can clearly see from the data, a committed marriage between one man and one woman is the best living arrangement on every level. If you want to be happier, healthier, more sexually satisfied, more prosperous, and more fulfilled in life, get married and remain faithful in your marriage. Marriage is good for us, not bad for us! Marriage is an extreme advantage! It was God's idea to bless each of us! It is important to note that the vast majority of the studies I have reviewed indicate that those couples who view each other as *best friends* indicate higher levels of overall satisfaction and well-being than those who indicate that they are not friends with their spouse. This difference should be understandable for obvious reasons. It should also give us greater reason to work on the keys we have outlined in this book to help you create a deeper friendship with each other.

The truth about divorce rates

And contrary to popular belief, divorce is much less common than we've been led to think. I have a great deal of respect for researcher and author Shaunti Feldhahn, who reported in a recent book that four out of five marriages are happy and that "the actual average is 80 percent: 80 percent of marriages are happy." In addition she states, "The studies show that if they stay married for five years, that almost 80 percent of those will be happy five years later." Feldhahn's book *The Good News about Marriage* also reveals that the divorce rate among Christians active in their church is 27 to 50 percent lower than divorce rates among non-churchgoers.[19]

Of course, marriage does not *guarantee* that you will experience all these benefits, nor does it guarantee that you will not have problems, poverty, difficulties, or challenges. But I want to make it clear that what God designed in marriage is good and a blessing to our lives, regardless of our circumstances, and it is worth your every effort to protect and preserve your marriage!

Notes

Introduction

1. Jay L. Zagorsky, Center for Human Resource Research, Ohio State University. "US data from the National Longitudinal Survey of Youth (NLSY79), which surveyed individuals in their 20s, 30s, and early 40s, shows that over time single respondents slowly increase their net worth but married respondents experience per person net worth increases of 77 percent over single respondents. Additionally, their wealth increases on average 16 percent for each year of marriage. Divorced respondents' wealth starts falling four years before divorce and they experience an average wealth drop of 77 percent.

2. David Leonhardt, "Marriage, Baby Carriage and Poverty," *New York Times*, June 28, 2017, https://www.nytimes.com/2017/06/28/opinion/millennials-marriage-children-poverty.html.

3. Joseph Lupton and James P. Smith, "Marriage, Assets, and Savings," Rand Corporation (November 1999), http://www.rand.org/pubs/drafts/DRU2215.html. "Those who became and stayed married tended to have much higher personal net worth than their peers. Being or becoming single had the opposite effect."

4. Vishal Mangalwadi, *Truth and Transformation: A Manifesto for Ailing Nations* (Seattle: YWAM Publishing, 2009), 47–53.

Chapter One: Key #1 Commit to Becoming a Peacemaker

1. Stephanie Jacques, "Researcher finds correlation between financial arguments, decreased relationship satisfaction," Kansas State University News Release (July 12, 2013), www.k-state.edu/media/newsreleases/jul13/predictingdivorce71113.html.

2. Ibid.

3. Ibid.

4. Institute for Divorce Financial Analysts, https://www.institutedfa.com/Leading-Causes-Divorce/.

5. Ibid.

6. C. S. Lewis, *Mere Christianity*, from the chapter titled "Christian Marriage."

7. DalyFocus blog by Jim Daly, Focus on the Family, January 12, 2015, jimdaly.focusonthefamily.com/what-we-can-learn-from-president-george-h-w-and-barbara-bushs-marriage/.

8. Claire Cain Miller, "Study Finds More Reasons to Get and Stay Married," *New York Times*, January 8, 2015, www.nytimes.com/2015/01/08/upshot/study-finds-more-reasons-to-get-and-stay-married.html?r=0.

Chapter Two: Key #2 Grasp the Biblical Definition of Prosperity

1. "5Cs," Uniquely Singapore, http://uniquelysingapore.org/5cs/.

2. John Piper, *Don't Waste Your Life* (Wheaton, IL: Crossway, 2003), 112.

Chapter Three: Key #3 Know and Fulfill Your Life Purpose

1. Nick Vujicic bio, Life Without Limbs ministry website, https://www.lifewithoutlimbs.org/about-nick/bio/.

2. Westminster Shorter Catechism, http://www.opc.org/sc.html.

3. Dr. Bill Bright, "God's Will for Your Life (The Paul Brown Letter)," www.cru.org/train-and-grow/spiritual-growth/the-paul-brown-letter.html.

4. Michelle Ule, "Oswald and Biddy Chambers' Solemn Promise," michelleule.com, November 19, 2013, http://www.michelleule.com/2013/11/19/st-pauls-cathedral-solemn-promise/.

5. David McCasland, *Oswald Chambers: Abandoned to God* (Grand Rapids: Discovery House Publishers, 1998), 148–49.

6. Ibid.

7. https://archon.wheaton.edu/?p=creators/creator&id=198.

8. http://www.oswaldchambers.co.uk/bio/.

Chapter Four: Key #4 Live by God's Philosophy of Money

1. Erika Rawes, "Top Five Money Problems Americans Face," The Wall Street Cheat Sheet, September 2014, *USA Today*, www.usatoday.com/story/money/personalfinance/2014/09/20/wall-st-cheat-sheet-money-problems-15832929/.

2. Angela Correll, Not Quite Amish blog, http://notquiteamishliving.com/2014/01/debt-is-bad-saving-is-good/.

3. Dr. Paul Chappell, "Establishing Financial Purpose," *Daily in the Word*, June 8, 2010, http://www.dailyintheword.org/content/establishing-financial-purpose.

4. Angela Correll, "Keeping it simple: Money matters and words from the heart," January 9, 2014, http://notquiteamishliving.com/2014/01/debt-is-bad-saving-is-good/.

Chapter Five: Key #5 Understand and Respect Your Spouse's Personality

1. Brittany C. Solomon and Joshua J. Jackson, "The Long Reach of One's Spouse," *Psychological Science*, October 17, 2014, journals.sagepub.com/doi/abs/10.1177/0956797614551370?rss=1&.

2. Andrew O'Connell, "The One Thing About Your Spouse's Personality

That Really Affects Your Career," *Harvard Business Review*, March 2015, https://hbr.org/2014/11/the-one-thing-about-your-spouses-personality-that-affects-your-career.

3. Brittany C. Solomon and Joshua J. Jackson, "The Long Reach of One's Spouse."

4. Rachael Rettner, "Want a Lasting Marriage? Personality Match May Not Matter," *Live Science*, August 11, 2011, www.livescience.com/15511-lasting-marriage-personality-match-matter.html.

Chapter Six: Key #6 Create a Unified Financial Plan

1. "A Journey Out of Debt," video, 6:34, Fox Business, December 29, 2010, http://video.foxbusiness.com/v/4477804/?#sp=show-clips.

2. Quinten Fottrell, "How One Couple Wiped Out a $125,000 Debt," *Market Watch*, February 14, 2015, http://www.marketwatch.com/story/how-one-couple-wiped-out-a-125000-debt-2014-06-27.

3. Sheryl Nance-Nash, "How to Slay Your Debt Demon: Two Families Share Secrets for Getting Rid of $100,000," *Forbes*, April 3, 2012, https://www.forbes.com/sites/sherylnancenash/2012/04/03/how-to-slay-your-debt-demon-two-families-share-secrets-for-gettng-rid-of-90000-100000/#68a7a1393a4b.

4. "Family is Out of Debt and Thankful," *FamilyMeans* (blog), September 22, 2013, https://www.familymeans.org/blog/articles/2013/09/22/family-is-out-of-debt-and-thankful.

5. "After Paying Off Six Figure Debt, Couple Celebrates Five Years of Remaining Debt Free," The National Foundation for Credit Counseling (NFCC), https://www.nfcc.org/press_hidden/multimedia/news-releases/after-paying-off-six-figure-debt-couple-celebrates-five-years-of-remaining-debt-free/.

Chapter Eight: Marriages That Give Us All Hope

1. Charlie and Dotty Duke share more of their testimony in their book *Moonwalker* (Nashville: Thomas Nelson, 1990).

Appendix: A Case for Marriage and Families

1. Maggie Gallagher, "Why Marriage Is Good for You," *City Journal Magazine*, Autumn 2000, www.city-journal.org/html/why-marriage-good-you-12002.html.

2. Lee Kuan Yew, "Warning Bell for Developed Countries: Declining Birth Rates," *Forbes*, October 16, 2012, http://www.forbes.com/sites/currentevents/2012/10/16/warning-bell-for-developed-countries-declining-birth-rates/#499eb0e1ea5f.

3. Cecilie Wehner, Mia Kambskard, and Peter Abrahamson, "Demography of the Family—The Case of Denmark," University of York, https://www.york.ac.uk/inst/spru/research/nordic/denmdemo.PDF.

4. Frank Newport and Joy Wilke, "Desire for Children Still Norm in U.S.," Gallup, September 25, 2013, http://www.gallup.com/poll/164618/desire-children-norm.aspx.

5. "Dropping birth rates threaten global economic growth," CBS Money-Watch, May 7, 2014, http://www.cbsnews.com/news/dropping-birth-rates-threaten-global-economic-growth/.

6. Ibid.

7. Leslie Ford, "Does Marriage Make You Happier? What a New Study Found," February 12, 2015, *Daily Signal*, http://dailysignal.com/2015/02/12/marriage-make-happier-new-study-found/.

8. David Leonhardt, "Marriage, Baby Carriage and Poverty," *New York Times*, June 28, 2017, https://www.nytimes.com/2017/06/28/opinion/millenials-marriage-children-poverty.html.

9. Augustine Reyes Chan, "Is the Secret to Wealth Getting Married?", February 23, 2015, http://nextshark.com/is-the-secret-to-wealth-getting-married/, emphasis added..

10. Jay L. Zagorsky, "Marriage and Divorce's Impact on Wealth," *Journal of Sociology*, December 1, 2005, http://journals.sagepub.com/doi/abs/10.1177/1440783305058478?journalCode=josb.

11. Bryan Caplan, "What Is the Male Marriage Premium?", Library of Economics and Liberty, February 28, 2012, http://econlog.econlib.org/archives/2012/02/what_is_the_mar.html.

12. The mean net worth of married couple households ($187,102) was substantially higher than that of cohabitant households ($77,093), male-headed households ($92,045), and female-headed households ($48,726), which was the lowest of all family structures. Michael Grinstein-Weiss, Yeong Hun Yeo, Min Zhan, and Charles Pajarita, "Asset Holding and Net Worth among Households with Children: Differences by Household Type," *Children and Youth Services Review* 30 (2008): 62–78.

13. Data from the random U.S. sample generated by the National Health and Social Life Survey (NHSLS) in 1994 provide information about population studies of sexual satisfaction (Laumann, Gagnon, Michael, & Michaels, 1994). Given the amount of critical comments made about the quality or frequency of sex in marriage and other committed relationships, the data support the idea of contented partners. A large majority (88%) of married individuals reported feeling extremely or very satisfied with their physical relationship and having feelings of love after engaging in sexual behaviors. Married respondents, especially those who were monogamous, reported the highest levels of sexual satisfaction, whereas cohabiting and dating couples reported slightly lower levels of satisfaction. www.sexscience.org.

14. Singles saved less money ($6,000–$6,500) over an eight-year period (between 1984–1989 and 1989–1994) than married couples did. J. Lupton, *Marriage and the Economy: Theory and Evidence from Advanced Industrial Societies* (Cambridge, UK: Cambridge University Press, 2003), 129–52.

15. On average, married-couple families accumulate significantly more assets than female-headed households. The level of assets in married-couple households (both financial and nonfinancial) was nearly four times as great as the level of assets for female-headed households. Martha N. Ozawa and Yongwoo Lee, "The Net Worth of Female-Headed Households: A Comparison to Other Types of Households," *Family Relations* 55, No. 1 (January 2006): 132–45.

16. Marriage is associated with lower mortality risk. Over the course of eight years, the odds of mortality were 58 percent higher for never-married individuals, 27 percent for divorced/separated individuals, and 39 percent for widowed individuals, compared to married individuals. Robert M. Kaplan and Richard G. Kronick, "Marital Status and Longevity in the U.S. Population," *Journal of Epidemiology and Community Health* 60, No. 9 (September 2006): 760–65.

17. On average, married couples are less likely than cohabiting couples to be in poverty. The income-to-needs ratios, which measure family economic resources (family income divided by poverty threshold), were higher for married men and women than for cohabiting couples. The likelihood that married couples were in poverty was 9 to 11 percent lower compared to cohabiting couples. Sarah Avellar and Pamela J. Smock, "The Economic Consequences of the Dissolution of Cohabiting Unions," *The Journal of Marriage and Family* 67, No. 2 (May 2005): 315–27.

18. According to a new study, men with kids earned a median salary of $49,000, while men without kids earned a median salary of $29,000. Men with kids also earned twice as much as women with children. Jeffrey Strain, "It's Financially Good to Be a Father, Dads Earn 41 Percent More Than Childless Men," SavingAdvice.com, http://www.savingadvice.com/articles/2014/10/14/1029083_dads-earn-more-than-childless-men.html.

19. Shaunti Feldhahn received her research training at Harvard. She and her husband, Jeff, help people with their marriages and relationships through bestselling books like *For Women Only*, *For Men Only*, and *The Good News About Marriage*. Shaunti reveals that the actual divorce rate has never gotten close to 50 percent. Those who attend church regularly have a significantly lower divorce rate than those who don't, and most marriages are happy. Shaunti Feldhahn, *The Good News About Marriage* (Colorado Springs: Multnomah, 2014), http://www.shaunti.com/book/good-news-marriage/.

Acknowledgments

A BOOK IS THE result of the efforts and influence of many people, all of whom are vital to the success of the project. While we each have hopes that many people will be served by the impact and ministry of the book, unfortunately, the author will often get far too much of the credit as those testimonies are received. To those below who have made this book possible, I pray that any good results derived by the people who read and apply the keys in this book will accrue to your eternal credit for all you have done to make it possible. Truly, you deserve as much credit and appreciation as the author.

First, to my wonderful wife, Ann; you fulfill the promise found in Proverbs 12:4: "A wife of noble character is her husband's crown . . ." Not only did you shape the entire content of the book over the course of our marriage, you agreed to be my ghostwriter to help me complete the manuscript and ensure my words accurately reflected our own story; and you generally encouraged me during the many long days of sitting at the keyboard typing alone. I thank you, my love. I know that many women who read our story will be grateful for your patient, strong, wise, and loving example to them.

Our children, Hank and Lindsay, Todd, John, and Luke deserve our sincere appreciation for your grace and mercy during our times of inadequacy as your parents. We have dedicated this book to you and our grandchildren in hopes it will be an inspiration and guide for you in years to come.

Thank you to Jorge Nishimura, my friend and partner in ministry in Brazil. It was your invitation to speak to families on financial issues "beyond the budget" that caused me to formulate these seven keys into a talk. You also allowed me to present this material live at University of the Family's annual conference. These acts encouraged me to make the effort to write the book in hopes of helping more families. You and Marcia are a great example to me of a marriage that God has blessed.

Thank you, Ingrid Beck, our acquisitions editor at Moody Publishers. You deserve significant credit for your willingness to take on our project. Your tireless, patient efforts helped us to move the original concept from a lot of words that looked to you like a bowl of spaghetti to a readable manuscript worthy of publication. May God bless you and give you the desires of your heart.

Thank you, Betsey Newenhuyse, for your outstanding work as editor. Your discerning eye and very keen insights moved the book to a new level of impact with far greater potential to be an enduring tool that will help marriages for years to come.

To Ashley Torres and Janis Todd and the Moody marketing team, your marketing efforts have been invaluable. I am so grateful to have had you on our team for the book launch.

Thank you to the incredible team I have the privilege of serving with at Crown Financial Ministries: Bob Dickie, Handre de Jongh, Sheila Thompson, Wayne Everbach, Tracey Fries, and Heather Stanfield, each of whom contributed to, encouraged, and shaped this book.

About the Authors

CHUCK BENTLEY joined Crown Financial Ministries in 2000 and was unanimously selected by the Board of Directors to serve as the CEO in 2007. He is only the third CEO of the ministry, preceded by the founder, Larry Burkett (1976–2000), and Howard Dayton (2000–2007).

Chuck has traveled throughout the world teaching biblical financial principles to the affluent, middle class, poor, and ultra-poor. He is the author of four books, including his most recent, *The Worst Financial Mistakes in the Bible and How You Can Avoid Them*. He is the executive producer of the God Provides™ Film Learning Experience. These films are now in thirty languages with the potential to reach two billion oral and visual learners. He writes and produces a daily radio broadcast heard on over 1,200 outlets in the United States. In 2011, he founded the Christian Economic Forum, which has convened marketplace leaders from more than twenty-five nations.

Chuck is a frequent guest speaker addressing both churches and business leaders on biblical financial topics. He has appeared on many television, radio, and news outlets around the world.

Chuck and his wife, Ann, have been married since 1978. Both are graduates of Baylor University. Ann is mother to four boys and also adores her four grandchildren. She has previous experience in banking, retail, and education. She currently devotes much of her time to homeschooling her two youngest sons. She also loves mentoring young women and leading a small group through Bible Study Fellowship (BSF). Her passions and hobbies include spending time in the Bible, piano, reading, gardening, and knitting.

Chuck and Ann have traveled together to five continents seeking to advance Crown's mission. They currently live in Knoxville, Tennessee.

About Crown Financial Ministries

CROWN FINANCIAL MINISTRIES serves people worldwide seeking to improve their personal finances, businesses, and careers. We also serve those considered among the world's poorest through the Crown Stewardship Training Center in Malawi, Africa. Through the Christian Economic Forum, launched in 2011, we seek to serve and inspire global leaders who embrace and practice God's financial principles.

Crown, formerly known as Christian Financial Concepts, was founded in 1976 by the late Larry Burkett, as a nonprofit educational ministry. Headquartered in Knoxville, Tennessee, today Crown has operations in cities across the United States and active outreach in over one hundred nations across five continents.

Crown offers a variety of resources, including books, online content, video, radio, podcasts, seminars, small-group studies, and dramatic films, as well as conferences and personal help. Our mission is accomplished through a global network of dedicated staff and volunteers, plus over fifty partnerships and alliances.

We invite you to get acquainted with us. It is our privilege to serve you.

crown.org

 CROWN

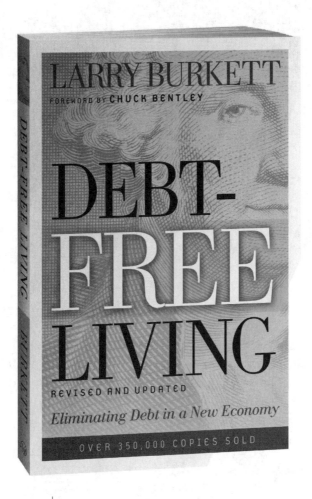

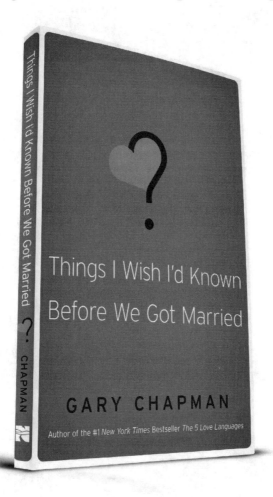